Dear Stinkpot

Letters
from
Louise Brooks

Dear Stinkpot

Letters from Louise Brooks

Or, My Education With LULU

Jan Wahl

BearManor Media
2010

Dear Stinkpot: Letters From Louise Brooks
© 2010 Jan Wahl

For information, address:

BearManor Media
P. O. Box 71426
Albany, GA 31708

bearmanormedia.com

Cover design by John Teehan

Typesetting and layout by John Teehan

Published in the USA by BearManor Media

ISBN—1-59393-474-2
978-1-59393-474-3

Table of Contents

To two beloved friends

Mogens Gad,
Copenhagen

and

Barbara Lucas,
Madison, NJ

Foreword

word

When Louise Brooks died in 1985, James Card, the curator of the film archive at Eastman House said of her, "She was an enormously powerful individual, thinker, and searcher for the absolute essence of things. I think she'd like to be remembered for her writing rather than for her films." I totally agree, and find it tragic that she never completed her autobiography or wrote her memoirs. What she left behind was a collection of essays, LULU IN HOLLYWOOD, done in what film historian Peter Cowie called "stunning prose." Sadly, all we had were those eight stunning essays, that is, until now.

In this book, Jan Wahl gives us a picture of Louise Brooks heretofore never seen. The intimate letters contained in this volume cover a poignant, rare, and sometimes volatile twenty-year friendship. Although much has been written about Louise Brooks, she reveals here for the first time unique facets of her personality. Always composing in a white heat of emotion and inspiration (occasionally fueled by gin), Jan states that her thoughts were "whimsical, profound, irritating, and sublime."

The story of their relationship, as told in these letters and commentary, is the story of two fledgling writers honing their craft. They were growing and learning together, nurturing each other. One struggling beyond her prime, and the other not yet having achieved it.

My interest in raven-haired Louise Brooks began long ago when I was a youngster. My other favorite was ash-blonde Ann Harding. These two ladies fired my romantic film imagination. They were flip sides of the same coin. Ann has always been my Angel of Light, and Louise my Dark Angel.

In March of 1990 Jan Wahl published an article about his friendship with Louise in *The Toledo Blade*. I read it, totally elated and excited to learn a fellow Toledoan had actually known Louise Brooks! I was determined to meet this man, and find out more about my Dark Angel.

I met Jan Wahl in 1991 when he was signing his latest children's book, TAILYPO. I introduced myself, confessing I wasn't really familiar with his work, but wanted to talk about Louise Brooks. He smiled, and we instantly became friends. I'm convinced his career as an author in some small way, or perhaps in a large way, was jump-started by the friendship with Louise, as her letters and his commentary will show. I urge you to read his THROUGH A LENS DARKLY and BEAR DANCE (inspired by Louise) and the collected short stories, YOUTH'S MAGIC HORN, dedicated to her.

Some readers may ask, "Why another book about Louise Brooks?" The answer is simple: "Why not?" These seminal documents penetrate more deeply into the mystery of Louise Brooks. This book confirms James Card's belief that her real calling was to be a writer. And it proves her number one love was writing. She sought truth through writing, which brought her great happiness in those last years. DEAR STINKPOT adds an important piece of the puzzle and enigma that is Louise Brooks. Yet, ironically, establishes that her mystery can never be totally solved. As the great American Master, Ray Bradbury, has said: "Everything ends in mystery."

– Sigmund Humanski
Toledo, Ohio 2009

Introduction

Imagine willingly throwing away Youth and Fame! They became demons for Louise Brooks, who struggled to release them.

Her letters are proof of the arduous journey Louise undertook and reveal her anger, her inner turmoil, her intelligence, and at the end she was victorious.

She may have imagined many wrongs and we must forgive her for ones she inflicted upon others. I try not to judge.

I've made a selection from a period of 20 years. A few are slightly edited. I have left the misspellings to show that she wrote at white heat; her fingers flew over the keys. In 1982, her *LULU in Hollywood* was published to great acclaim. I have had some success in writing for children. She would shout at me, "Dammit! Grow up!" but if I'd followed this advice I'd be out of business. Ultimately the child in me has been my strength.

Between each of her letters I chose, I explain names or situations as well as to bring my own life in focus. We each were growing as writers and fed off each other. She was a major education for me while I endeavored to give support as well or to send small gifts to please her. She sent walnut fudge.

How I wish Louise lived long enough to know *Bear Dance*, published in 2008—my fable inspired by her. Bear dances freely in the forest and on the meadow, until caught and shackled by humans who make him dance to their tune.

Any writer has got to be an observer or a floating camera. Out of necessity a writer is an outsider. Perhaps this outsider aspect is what drew Louise and me together.

By 1955, Louise had withdrawn to a tiny flat in Rochester, thanks to an invitation from James Card, Curator of Motion Pictures at George Eastman House, and to a stipend from William Paley. Our introduction was in the city of Copenhagen. Card had brought her there as a stopover on the way to Paris.

We met at the office of Ove Brusendorff, head of the Danish Film Museum. Ove's claim to fame was as compiler of a monumental work on sex.

Earlier that same year, 1957, I'd been serving as amanuensis to Isak Dinesen on her *Last Tales.* One terrible morning I was summarily dismissed by the great lady.

Explosion! "You have no feeling whatsoever for literature!" she decided. I had made two errors in three hours.

I loved Copenhagen. Being penniless I'd already sold my return ticket to Toledo. One silver gray evening I wandered on a long walk from the center of the city to Frederiksberg.

It was about eleven o'clock. At random I pressed a doorbell. I could not afford to stay at my modest pension hotel another night. A bundle of freckles answered my ring.

She told me in English, "Come in! This is your home." And it was, instantly. The following week, I was taken by ambulance to the hospital. Nervous exhaustion brought on by the ordeal with Isak Dinesen. The great writer was too much for my blood. Fortunately I was sheltered by the kindly Hallings, who became my new family.

I had no official work permit yet was briefly employed by one, then another Danish newspaper. My "job" was to translate reports from Viet Nam, from French into Danish. France was involved in that unhappy country. This before JFK sent to war fifty thousand "advisers."

My clumsy French was rendered into clumsier Danish, resulting in news items unlike those of any other paper in Denmark. I was let go.

Thanks to Ove Brusendorff I won a berth at the Film Museum. For a modest sum I labored in the stills department and wrote articles for the magazine *Kosmorama* and program notes for films.

Interesting visitors filtered through the office of Herr Brusendorff. Once it was Ingmar Bergmen, along with Harriet Andersson in tow. I was mesmerized by his teeth, which grew sideways. I kept staring at them and can't remember a single thing he said. I told him I was planning to do a book about Danish director Carl Theodor Dreyer and I would call it *Through A Lens Darkly.*

That I recall because those cigarette-stained teeth gleamed dimly at me. In 1961 Bergman made THROUGH A GLASS DARKLY.

On another day in huffed and puffed 300-pound Raymond Rohauer, with an elderly Hal Roach behind him. I had had problems with Rohauer, the scallywag of film collecting. I stepped away. From the next room I could hear him claiming he had rights to certain titles (he did not). He left with many prints which Brusendorff handed over.

Then, wonder of wonders, there was Jim Card and the legendary Louise Brooks. I knew Card and so was asked to escort them in grown-up style off to the Hotel d'Angleterre. Practically farm fresh, I was shocked that they intended now to share the room. The clerk at the desk did not bat an eye. He didn't know Jim was married to a saintly woman.

Jim's wonderful wife was able to grasp the bigger picture and was able to view Louise Brooks as someone out of film history. Actually the Card-Brooks connection was a brief one, not more than two years.

But when I next visited in Rochester I was witness to a duel of cooks. In her modest kitchen Louise at noon concocted a veritable feast while in the evening his wife whipped up a gala dinner. Mr. Card's waistline expanded.

Nevertheless Jim never lost his charm. Mary Pickford and Gloria Swanson were among his admirers. When they came to Eastman House they were treated as royalty.

Card amused himself by wearing a Nazi stormtrooper cap and drove a 1936 bullet-proof Mercedes owned by Josef Goebbels. He was no one to fool with, as Louise was to learn.

His book *Seductive Cinema* is both fascinating and irritating. Too bad he didn't write and lecture more and not manipulate people as if they were players in his screenplay.

James Card was lucky to have a magnificent wife. I was proud to call her a friend. So with some trepidation I encountered Louise and thus began our own roller-coaster friendship.

And Louise remained in Rochester to the close of her life. She was near enough to Eastman House to view the films of the past including her own. And she could receive her ecstatic worshippers as Jim helped rekindle interest in the legend.

Although a "recluse," Louise enjoyed the attention, to be sure. She shared gin with a growing number of Catholic priests who courted her. And her contemporaries such as Richard Arlen came to town. This is when I entered the scene—at the very moment news spread that she, Lulu, of G. W. Pabst's masterpiece *Pandora's Box*, was among the living.

We were two writers learning our craft together. Over the next decades I had a hundred tantalizing epistles from her, plus handwritten notes and cards, and, now and then, an urgent telegram.

Alas, I did not save all. I moved to Mexico and almost any communication she sent after that was lost.

The Card-Brooks sojourn to Denmark occurred in the fall of 1957.

The next year I returned to the States, again as a student, to finish my Master's. There would be trips to Rochester when I could afford them. By trial and error I realized it might be safer to keep Louise Brooks at arm's length.

I spent one night with her. But I was too young and she was too old.

1958

Tuesday February 25 1958
2155 East Avenue
Rochester NY

Dear Jan

If you care to be my pen pal, I'll thank you not to write on both sides of that thin paper.

It is bad about your heart, but then it might have the effect of getting you to work while there is yet light. Have you noticed that a foreshadowing of night gets things done? Van Gogh, Mozart. While it took Goethe 50 years to finish Faust. So much for cheering you up.

So much con in your letter, you bad boy. And encouraging me to write after making that distressed face when asked how you like my piece in *Image*.

We are going down to my dear New York which I hate for Thursday till Saturday. And I shall see Glennon I hope and find out "how's tings" and get a leveling off. Glennon is very good at that, being truthful, as hard on his friends as he is on himself.

Jimmie balked like a llama at going to see Mr. Pabst. As usual, he made up a thousand sage reasons. The truth being that he is shy, jealous, and hates getting second billing. For myself, I am not shy.

Now of course, he is sorry. It was for him that I wanted to go. What a lot he could have learned from Mr. Pabst. So useful in writing. And Jim is writing better all the time. SIGHT AND SOUND is using a Louise Brooks article by him in their july issue. I must pound his big fat head and get him to work on it.

Best love
Louise

In 1958, by spring I regained my health, after the trauma caused by Isak Dinesen's wrath. And the Baroness sent to Toledo one of the splendid Rie Nissen photo portraits of her as Pierrot. I rushed downtown to Lamson Bros. Store to show it off to Miss Helen Tiffany, the book seller.

In a separate 9x12 stamped manila envelope I had a story I was submitting someplace. Horror of horrors. Absentmindedly, I dropped my envelope with photo into the mailbox and brought the manuscript one into Lamson's. Miraculously, on the very next day, our mailman delivered to my parents' address the precious envelope containing the photo. There were no identifying markings of any kind.

As for Louise's letter you just read:

Image was a publication of George Eastman House. I don't recall the gist of the piece. My intention was to praise her, however I made a booboo. She needed judicious fine-tuning. And I took it upon myself to do the job.

But Louise was not keen on hearing how any of the wrinkles might be smoothed out. After all, a critic once insisted that she "needed no directing," her art was so pure.

Even the great G. W. Pabst, the director of her two German classics from the late Twenties, *Pandora's Box* and *Diary of a Lost Girl*, never attempted to direct her. He simply created an atmosphere for her.

When Card and Brooks went to Paris, she urged Jim to take her on to Vienna to meet Pabst whom she adored. She always pronounced "Mister Pabst" in a special way. Jim, of course, did not wish to share her with Pabst particularly. So, no Vienna.

Brooks's reputation as an actress is based on the two films by Pabst as well as on her 1930 French film *Prix de Beauté*—from an idea by René Clair (who was originally to have directed). Her voice was dubbed in the latter, also in the 1929 *The Canary Murder Case*, her final Paramount vehicle.

Louise did not have to speak to catch our attention.

Jim's *Sight and Sound* piece was entitled "The Intense Isolation of LOUISE BROOKS."

Thursday March 20 1958
2195 East Avenue
Rochester NY

Dear Jan

This morning, as it has been on so many other mornings, getting up with that yearning to DO SOMETHING, I thought I would work on a short story, PICKUP ON THIRD AVENUE. But along with dawn and a shower and coffee and crow's cawing, I decided to look up an agent who had told me to send such stuff to her. I searched through every phone book I'd kept from 1943. Evidently I had no faith in her for I didn't find any name but Shapiro on 57th that seemed possible. What I did find though were failures and humiliations of 15 years. Hundreds of names having to do with nothing but some hopeless attempt at work.

Whatever you do Jan, do not permit yourself to fail. The terrible effect of failure is reflected most clearly in people who have not failed. Like a person to whom God has given excellent health, the person who has not failed, ditch digger or business man, considers your failure a case of dogging it. "See what he has done!"

Failure might be best explained by a reasoning baby. "I crawl and cling and try to stand up and walk and all I do is stagger and stumble and bang my head and fall on my ass, so I'll give up trying to walk. I'll take to swimming, or flying, or making myself some prop."

So if you truly love to write. . .WRITE WRITE WRITE. A thousand rejections add up to experience, learning your trade. And unless you are extraordinarily fortunate, no one will know that you are good till you have made it.

That makes me think of Langlois. Never in my life have I known anyone whom I so much love and admire. He built this whole film archive thing from his own will and imagination. No money, no name, no background. But such strength and perseverance! And somehow I think that the next important thing is one's relations with people. I notice that Henri allows people neither to puff him up or pull him down. Like Lao Tzu, he is a calm flowing river between conflicting banks. Perhaps, if it doesn't kill him, he is right to become so fat. It holds him down. For a passionate man he is, with a strong temper.

Remember all the fights in Copenhagen? In Paris none. Like the night Jimmie wanted to dine in some dreary little joint on the left Bank, *I*, in Paris. Henri settled on a restaurant on the isle. To laugh is a wonderful thing.

Henri was, of course, Henri Langlois of the Cinémathèque Française. The Museum of Modern Art Film Library and the British Film Institute had sponsors. Langlois had to store his first collection of 35mm very inflammable nitrate prints in his bathtub.

This mutual admiration, Louise-Henri, was an odd one. Or was it?

Louise worshipped Herr Pabst. In 1929 he warned her she'd be unable to fit into Hollywood after Germany. And awakened in her something that caused the end of her movie career.

Henri Langlois and Jim Card worshipped a youthful pure image of

Louise. Card and Langlois saved her films; in those she was the dream star forever.

It's all mixed together: Louise, Pabst, Card, Langlois.

Thymian living the high life. *Diary of a Lost Girl* (1929)

Monday, March 24 1958

And Henri's wonderful eyes. Strange how the eyes of marvelously perceptive people stick out just enough to catch the light of every thought and transition. The proudest he made me was, after he was here, asking for a pientre Chinoise, une fleur, un oiseu. I just mailed one of my oils on mounting board to him. When I sketched the thing last year I had no idea what it was. But a letter and the sketch to the U of R brought word that I had painted Spanish thistle.

Letters to a stranger. I get up determined to write on a piece, give up, taking out my pleasure in writing to an intelligent stranger.

It's no fun writing to some one who knows you well, or one who doesn't understand, or some one who doesn't read. My sister, for one, who was brought up in one of those fancy French schools, Chateau de Grolav, from where I got nothing but bills for fancy dress, oils for painting, and eggs for souffle—she answers my letters as if she reads them through the envelope.

The well known friend knows you too well for dramatizing your self in the heroic manner. Or perhaps it is that they know that you know them too well—you don't go on saying those sweet flattering things that bring response.

And speaking of this Jan—either you didn't read the Image article very carefully or I write as badly as I think.

"She played by instinct alone, ignorant as hell of the great director's intentions."

The whole point of my admiration for Mr. Pabst was that he directed each actor on the actor's plane. With me it was some extrasensatory transmission. He is the exact opposite of Henri —— a sender, not a receiver.

There is such a need for good writers in TV, in radio. You know your chances of making money in books, or even magazines which are mostly staff written, are lousy.

And now, too, a TV writer winds up in pictures. Study them and see yourself a success.

You may, of course, dedicate your book to me —— but why?

> Best love
> Louise

Thursday March 20 and Monday March 24 were in the same envelope.

U of R is the University of Rochester which Louise sometimes used as a source for information.

Reminds me: school days.

It was Louise who prodded me to return to the University of Michigan for "higher education." My mentor there was eccentric critic Austin Warren. I love his *New England Saints.* In it, for instance, he reveals Ralph Waldo Emerson's Aunt Mary Moody went about on horseback in her shroud and, like Sarah Bernhardt, slept in her coffin.

At Cornell I had had the privilege of taking Creative Writing under Baxter Hathaway, editor of *Epoch* magazine. Like Louise, both professors have been constant guideposts.

Hathaway included one of my stories, "At the Crossing," in his *Best Short Stories Since WWII.* It was based on an actual happening. I was about five years of age. Grandpa Wahl, Great-Uncle Fred Lesh, the postmaster of Holgate, Ohio, and I were en route to a church banquet. Uncle Fred was driving. At the B & O crossing he failed to stop. The autopsy on Uncle Fred proved he had died of a heart attack before our car reached the tracks. As he slumped forward, his foot kept pressing against the pedal. The machine kept moving. Grandpa Wahl and I leaped out of the car in the nick of time before the train hit. The awful force of the impact sent Uncle Fred's body flying into the air.

This incident proved to me that fiction can't beat real life.

Did I mention Professor Warren was eccentric? On a hard winter night I braved a blizzard in Ann Arbor to keep an appointment. Austin Warren took my heavy coat, and then disappeared into a long, long closet for a full five minutes.

When he emerged, with my coat still in hand, he gave it to me declaring mysteriously, "It's been an illuminating session, hasn't it?

Another time—to paraphrase a poem by John Donne, the learned fellow shook his cane up at the ceiling and shouted, "Rape me, God!"

Amen.

2125 East Avenue
Rochester NY
Wednesday ? September 24 1958

Dear Jan

How sweet of you to send me THE EAGLE AND THE DOVE. Although, if she carries out the idea, I know I shan't agree with Virginia. Big St. Teresa was the belle of the ball before she went into the church. Little Therese was just like my sister, June (a convert before me—How I wish I had a copy of the letter I wrote her deploring her state), almost ten years younger than I, brought up mostly by me in French schools, Paris, she is a pure, good woman, as hard as cement. Like the priests, I find her unpleasant. That is one thing I wanted to tell you. How priests are the most fascinating and individual people. Ten months I was taking instruction. And we never got through the lessons. I would get Fr Egan or Fr Burkort off on art or literature or whatnot and two hours would pass without a book opened.

Whatever happens, I want you to throw off your false character, for good. You were so beautiful and gay before you left Rochester. That is what we were put in the world for. Did Christ leave so much as a written word? and Goethe wrote, "For a man remains of consequence, not so far as he leaves something behind him, but so far as he acts and enjoys, and rouses others to action and enjoyment."

After two operations, Jimmie's poor wife is going home Thursday, still blind in one eye. But he will be happy to have her and the children home again. He loved having you with him. He is not a lone person. That was our problem in Europe last year. I am not a family person. Most of the time I must be alone. Although I can live with anyone who does not ask me constantly to be amusing.

Jimmie convinced me that I should go to Paris. The Hommage a Louise Brooks is arranged for November 4.

Best love
Louise

Louise once informed me one reason she converted to the Catholic Church was not to be tempted with thoughts of suicide.

The Eagle and the Dove, a graceful study of French saint Thérèse and Spanish saint Teresa, one from Lieux, the other from Avila (I forget which is dove and which is eagle), was from the pen of Vita Sackville-West, onetime intimate of Virginia Woolf. I suspected this might be a volume to catch Louise's fancy. Sometimes my little gifts were the right ones.

And she attended the homage, a big-scale one this time, at the Cinémathèque. Without James Card. In Paris she was the Marilyn Monroe of silent pictures. To Henri Langlois, the critic Ado Kyrou, Card and others, Louise was the "Face of the Century."

On this trip she lacked a protector, however in Jim's absence she made a long-lasting bond with Langlois's assistant Lotte Eisner. While Eisner became a bosom pal, Mary Meerson, lover of Langlois and widow of set designer for René Clair, Lazare Meerson, became an antagonist. Meerson swore Louise was making a play for Henri.

What I remember about Mary Meerson was she had a habit of adding one dress over another, many, many dresses, until she resembled a tea cozy.

After the tiring international journey to France, Louise was ever cautious about leaving her snug nest again.

On Christmas Day to my joy I had a phone call from her; she was not going to travel anymore. Not for anything.

Or anybody.

1959

Saturday February 14 1959
2155 East Avenue
Rochester 10 NY

Junior!

I'm fat enough to look like candy, but how did you know I adore presents and that I am an old candy box collector from way back in 1911? And did Jimmie write to thank you for the Caligari and the frame which he adores? Now I have suggested that he get rid of the dinky crap in his office and put in a few stately pieces to match. This insult to his taste is holding up all change until he cools out. But he doesn't get nearly so mad as he used to — no blows!

We are going up to Toronto Friday for a Sunday showing of LULU. He is looking forward to it because his speech will be grand, naturally. His last effort I did not hear till closing night, although I was suspicious because he was so excited about the angry audience reaction. Well, Stinkie, it was crazy. Quoting that juvinile Agee, he read with such passion and so well that everyone thought he was speaking for himself—and so Nazi. Then he showed a pro-Jewish picture, MARRIAGE IN SHADOWS. It was a sloppy job that was unpardonable. He is too well known. The Dryden Theater is no longer a playpen I said. And just suppose I were an enemy? What a fool-making piece I could write about him. He is just as sharp in criticizing my work but I don't write fast and have time to clear my mind for corrections. And I can slink into the amateur writer class.

This morning working on Clara Bow in Photoplay I read a review (August 1931) of THREE LOVES, Terra, German silent about 1928, with Dietrich and Fritz Kortner. Did you ever hear of it? Have you seen Dietrich in I KISS YOUR HAND, MADAME? Same time — lovely. Jim has it. Oh, I must check my Chili con Carne.

And you wicked boy. Jimmie tells me you swung with a reel of CAMILLE. With a story too ridiculous not to be believed. Send it back, Jan, not for that lousy M of M A but for yourself. And write them the truth which will be such a shock to their self-interest and muddling lies that they will offer you a job.

When I was 18 from the library of Morgan Morgan (then the husband of Margaret Case Harriman) I took PORTRAIT OF A YOUNG MAN from the signed edition of George Moore. Everyone raised hell with me. I would admit nothing. The book made me miserable and I think I threw it away.

To preserve your special kind of beauty it is necessary to avoid lies and Oves.

Wednesday February 18 1959

Today, I am just as cross as Glennon was at me last week sending me obscene postcards in Latin, French and — "Viva Mary astor! Flesh like alabaster!/ Who could come faster? Can you play canasta?" But besides your gift, both he and Henri Langlois and Mr Pabst have written beautifully to me. What old broad — what young broad could ask for more? My trouble is, doubtless, that I must tell Jimmie that I won't go to Toronto. It is always so. Like making Mary furious about not going to Lausanne. Unless the debt is great, my first and last personal appearance is chalked up—Paris, 1958. Anyhow, I can't leave Suzy-cat. Jim gave her to me. She jumped in his car in front of a bar.

Now I am re-reading your December 31 letter. You won't hear from Greta. The only thing contemplative about her is the color of her hair. She is LIVING. Such people don't write people outside their lives. How I wish I were rich and could have asked her to Paris. I adore her. She suits me with her silence, her sulks (why do Danes and Swedes sulk so much?) and her naughtiness.

All these people you read I knew (not F P A). How can you write from them? A life you haven't experienced? You are either a true poet or a daydreaming, beguiled boy. Three hours a day I read about myself and the women I write about and the better I know me and them the more I have to learn. But then, as I said, I am strictly amateur.

You can have the loan of VANITY FAIR. How do you prepose perpose pupose to get them? Right now I am working on Jimmie to get a Clara Bow talkie without which I cannot begin my piece. (You know his magpie contrariness)

And for God's sake, Junior, don't be burying yourself again. What are you running from at 25? Copenhagen and now thoughts of Colorado Springs and that painting place Santa Fe in New Mexico. With a small allowance you can go to Paris and work at Cinémathèque and write and meet the most wonderful people in the world. They are gay, I mean gai, wise and kind and I have already prepared the way for you. For myself, Renoir and Man Ray were indiscribible experiences.

My article, except for the editor, Penelope Houston, lays lies? flat as my first omelet. Like my whole career. SI-LENCE. When I stopped dancing—rapturous. After the FOL-LIES—the most beautiful. Thirty years after LULU—suberb actress. Even you say nothing. About the SIGHT article.

Best love

Louise

A lot to explain on this one.

The tin painted candy box had a color portrait of Rudolph Valentino on the lid; it was circa 1922. I believe later I also gave her one with Gloria Swanson on it.

The *Caligari* was a rare lobby card. The frame was original stills from Carl Th. Dreyer's *Vampyr* made in 1932, given to me by Herr Dreyer the summer of 1954 on the set of *Ordet*, now considered one of his classics. I framed them in Copenhagen in 1957.

Jan Wahl and his "American godson," Ricky Rosenthal, Ann Arbor.
Photo by Robert Rosenthal.

LULU is Pabst's film with Louise, *Pandora's Box* (1928). Agee is James Agee, poet-film critic-screenwriter. His most remarkable script is for Charles Laughton's masterwork *Night of the Hunter* (1955), with Robert Mitchum, Shelley Winters and Lillian Gish.

Dryden Theater is the theater for George Eastman House. Card would give an illuminating, intelligent, crisp lecture to accompany each program.

Louise was working on her book *Thirteen Women,* never completed.

About the reel of *Camille*: at Cornell in 1953, as an undergraduate, I started a film group we called The Griffith Club. Some 16mm prints were from my collection, some we rented from Thomas J. Brandon or the Museum of Modern Art. The Garbo 1936 *Camille,* directed by George Cukor, was from MoMA. Following the showing, intoxicated by Garbo's lady of the camillias, we three officers crossed Triphammer Bridge over one of Ithaca's gorges. This, after a celebration at a pub called Johnny's Big Red.

Each of us balanced a 1600 foot 16mm unit on our head. Mine was Unit One. Giddy and careless, I—whoops—lost my reel. It tumbled from the suspension bridge in view of my buddies into whirling rapids.

Yes sir.

That night I stayed up to compose a contrite letter to the Museum. They decided it was a college prank but charged for lost footage. Marguerite Akermark shared the story with Jim Card who spread it far and wide. Very unfair. I said nothing when Jim disposed of films I had stored at George Eastman House to take Louise to Barcelona when she declared she had a hankering to see Antonio Gaudi's architecture.

The upside was: Louise insisted on meeting me in Copenhagen.

Glennon = Jimmie Glennon, who ran a hangout on Third Avenue, a favorite spot of Louise and of Bogart and Benchley.

Mary = Mary Meerson, the human tea cozy.

There was to have been a tribute to Louise in Lausanne but Jim knew he would not be lionized as he was by Ove (Brusendorff) in Copenhagen or by Henri (Langlois).

Renoir = Jean Renoir. FPA = Franklin P. Adams.

Louise gave me my pick. Either the Man Ray or a terrific water-color of her by the Hungarian Willy Pogany. I chose the latter. To my regret I never got it.

The Garbo and Gish article for *Sight and Sound* I cobbled together for Louise out of her own writing. Playing pre-editor, I had honed her style. She did not object.

I insisted *S & S's* Penelope Houston only credit Louise Brooks. The cheque for her, made out on Lloyds of London Bank Ltd, 263 Tottenham Court Road, was sent to me. It's for $72.63. That was $73.63 less $1.00 charge.

I have framed the receipt.

(handwritten)

Friday - Feb - 20 - 1959 -

Yesterday Jim told me that it is next Friday in Toronto.

He is angry now about UNDERWORLD, his new picture. I went opening night - He set Von Sternberg up with Dreyer, Griffith, Pabst, etc - in his speech - and then I saw the picture - Evelyn Brent was gorgeous as a sym-bol of Will - But, about to be riddled with machine gun bullets, she expressed that old Brent invitation at being asked to a dull party. The picture stunk - except for the first 3 reels -

However, Jimmie says it was the bad ad lib music played by the organist that loused it up - they loved it, ~~Saturday~~ - Wednesday night - now he said -

Well, they loved it ~~Saturday~~ - He ran a contrast picture - the first Warner's talkie - gangster - LIGHTS OF NEW YORK? - he is becoming a great show man - a good speech -

I am playing Segovia -

Gish just wrote Jim that all I wrote in S & S was true - proving that insight has nothing to do with experience or facts - so write your book - I have 24 oatmeal cookies in the ice box - why don't you come up and stay with Suzy next week-end

Louise

(handwritten)

Monday - Feb - 23 - 1959 -

Well, why not send this silly letter –
And I won't go to Toronto - But Jim is
playing dead dog since my Decline - By
cat - Same as Paris trip -

These two messages are odd ones.

Evelyn Brent's first starring role was opposite John Barrymore in 1917's *Raffles the Amateur Cracksman*. And she played the older sister in one of Louise's more successful Paramounts, *Love 'Em and Leave 'Em* (1926).

Brent was a stunner and made two important silent features, both by Josef Von Sternberg, *Underworld* and *The Last Command* She kept acting until 1948. No wonder Louise gnashed her teeth. In *Love 'Em and Leave 'Em,* Evelyn Brent had star billing.

Suzy is the cat.

Does Louise mean I should take care of her in the event Louise and Jim go to Toronto? However she insists she's not going after all. Thus I did not hop on a Greyhound from Toledo and get involved in a messy situation.

Friday March 20 1959
2155 East Avenue
Rochester 10 NY

Dear Jan

Had I loved you less, reading your work would have been my last wish. How many times when I was young were friendships spoiled by my indifference to young writers' work. A glamorous profession and money were really their chief objects. But you are on the level, aiming at the highest art; that of putting the mysterious, unique world of Jan Wahl down in lifeless little black symbols.

If you were madly in love with yourself like Scott Fitzgerald I could judge how well you brought one character to life and let me understand the world he lives in. As it is, I can say that the opening of VALEDICTORIAN and the end are beautiful. And in it is some lovely imagery. For the rest, the technique, the style requires the highest powers—making every sensation and mental observation of life immediate in writing. The question is whether style is not made by content. Proust began with exquisite style but it was not until what he had to write became more important that his fascinating world became visible to the rest of us. And always I was kept from quite believing your characters because you seemed to be re-writing your own truth. (What will the neighbors say?)

When Fitzgerald wrote that his mother had an ocean liner turned back in midstream such an impossibility only clarified the kind of silliness that his characters believed in.

The trouble is that you are far more intelligent than he. The critical spirit blurs your vision. When Peter said, "I will be a fool for Christ," he spoke for all art.

With that I shall finish by saying that nothing gives me the right to evaluate your work. These being my impressions, however, I know that you would rather have them than kind nothings or obvious hedging required by the ordinary writer.

When are you coming to Rochester? You don't need much money. Surely you can stay with Jimmie and eat around. Jimmie is showing ROBIN HOOD and giving one of his best and funniest lectures.

Lotte wrote from Paris that CINEMA 59 reprinted parts of my article with "some interesting stills." Gordon (foreign publications) in New York doesn't carry it. Did you ever hear of it?

Love
Brooksie

I intended to dedicate my novel *Dancing on the Shore* to Louise.

"The Valedictorian" was the first of its seven parts. This was to be what the Germans refer to as a bildungsroman, an "educational" novel; i.e., in the process, the main character grows up. Thomas Mann's *Felix Krull* (like mine, never completed) is one.

The time frame of the story was to be 1927 to 1930, noteworthy in Louise's life. *Dancing* concerned a small town American girl, Caroline Way, who wants to be a great dancer. Just as she graduates from high school, Isadora Duncan dies a horrible death in France.

The mother of Preston Sturges, Mary Desti, was the hand of fate. It was she who gave Isadora the shawl to wear in the chilly night air as the trail-blazing dancer (whose innovations in movement inspired Rodin and Matisse) climbed into an open car, a little model known as an Amilcar.

Books on Duncan get it wrong; they think it was a Bugatti; that she was with a new lover. The young man was an Amilcar salesman.

The car sped off. The scarf got entangled in the right rear wheel, and snapped her neck. Caroline Way is convinced the soul of Isadora enters her body.

This is a new, younger Isadora. Caroline embarks on picaresque adventures—runs off with gypsies, lives in a Bohemian compound in Chicago (after all, Prokoviev went to Chicago; he wrote *The Love for Three Oranges* there) and so on.

I planned a second novel, in which in Nazi Germany as a celebrated modern dancer she is caught in Hitler's dark web.

It was not to be.

Epoch printed "The Valedictorian" and Macmillan paid for an option. I completed six of seven sections, and then somehow mislaid my manuscript. Anyhow, Louise had not been encouraging.

Saturday March 28 1959
2155 East Avenue
Rochester 10 1959

Dear Jan

Jimmie brought your package up Thursday. "A chocolate Easter egg," I said till I got to the fine wrapping then, "A Russian Easter egg with rubies—" and then the sweet English china with its Dresden pattern and the secret flower inside like the Chinese——inside the bowl for the drinker to look at. I put it on the table on the copper plate, little Robert's first try at silver smithing, in front of Esky's (Swedish) French dice cup holding Townsend Martin's African doll under the painting of Man Ray and the Kansu tomb impression of Henri Langois. Here in my own United Nations with my Rochester gin bottle I can sit for hours looking at these things and, on the desk, Howard Wong's little brush holder with the iron red seals worn away by the thumb of some assiduous painter, the pen tray hysted from the Essex House, the Russian cigarette box given me long ago in 1927 by some little actress called Louise something. And on the coffee table Irish Jimmie D's

Japanese porcupine box, the shell butter dish from the Royal Monceau in memory of Albert, the perfect waiter who grew fond of me in spite of himself and only lost his poise once when he came in and found one of Lotte's pansies using my razor in the bathroom. Next to it Jimmie

Art photo by Alfred Cheney Johnston, New York City, 1924. Jan Wahl collection.

Card's $4-dollar watch ticking comfortably to the crucifix of Glennon from Dublin, Sir. And on the wall, the stunning aluminum picture frame made years before such things became fashionable by Hungarian Bill Turansky. How can I be lonely with these beautiful friends around me?

Easter Morning

Last Thursday too Jim brought up a letter from Lotte Eisner which made him sniker happily for she wrote, "Everybody here was very amazed by your article and its lucidity. I had to fight people who thought it was Jim who had written it for you because those idiots could not understand that a beautiful woman can also be intelligent." (It was she in her book, L'Ecran Demoniaque, after being introduced to me in Berlin in 1929, who wrote that I was beautiful — and stupid.)

Also, Jimmie told me, before the magazine came out Maggie Dent of the Movie vultures told him down in New York that "everybody" knew he wrote for me.

You see! What did I tell you! And *he* (with my full consent) has rewritten most of my piece for what he terms one of his most successful lectures. He has offered to type up my note books in order to gather in material but I can't bear to let the sum of about 800 hour's work out of my possession.

Naturally, I have repented criticizing your work— with all my heart. When *I* wrote a little story and Jimmie said it stunk (this does not follow because I include your poetic gift with my no talent) I had to give up because I was completely helpless in analizing my own work. So how can I criticize yours?

WHEN ARE YOU COMING TO ROCHESTER
I'll make you goodies——
Love
Louise

I was honored to be among the souvenirs that meant a lot to Louise.

Townsend Martin was a socialite, a scenario writer—along with Walter Wanger responsible for getting her contract at Paramount. He wrote the original story to her second vehicle, *An American Venus*, shot in late 1925, and released in January 1926. *Venus* had a sequence in two-strip Technicolor. It is one of the lost films, although by chance I found a copy of its trailer.

The only Wong I know of is Anna May Wong. Presumably Howard Wong was an artist.

"Eskie" = a Swedish baron, Karl von Bieck. He was called "The Eskimo" because his light blond hair resembled an Eskimo's fur cap.

Louise referred to Lotte Eisner's bravura study known in English as *The Haunted Screen*, dealing with Murnau, Pabst, Fritz Lang and others.

Maggie Dent from Chapel Hill was one of Jim Card's groupies.

Wednesday May 27 1959
2155 East Avenue
Rochester 10 NY

Dear Jan

Unlike most of my letters which are pre-written in my head, this one will have to write itself. Ever since you left town—Jim said Tuesday, May 12—I wanted to write you, but it is so difficult. When Jim said you left because of your headaches I let the matter drop there. Gradually, from the priests, I am learning to keep my mouth shut, especially with Jim since between us the truth is pretty well understood in a wordless fashion.

But you cannot know how sad your leaving made me —— as if I would never see you again.

From the beginning my impression was that you were deeply uneasy here and wanted to get away. Bored too, not having any fun. I had hoped to see a good deal of you, to laugh, to talk, to understand you better. Nothing worked out.

Bill Johnnes wrote me a lovely letter full of flattery. He is a good boy. I wrote Mike Hall in publicity at Paramount to see him and give him some plugs in the columns. Mike has been my "protege" since he was 21 in 1944, working his way up from a waiter at the Concord in the Catskills to his own publicity office. He got mad at me for a letter last October. But last week he wrote again, and instead of an allday sucker, sent me an item about my book in the Journal-American.

Thursday May 14 I had to go to dinner with Jim and Enrique Scheiby. In the whole world there cannot exist a person less to my liking. But keeping God and the good of Eastman House in mind, I concentrated on his superior understanding of pictures, and gave a fair performance. You will be amused to learn that the glitter in Jim's eye at the promise? of a brother in sex faded to absolute boredom.

The funniest tale of all was about the Sunday pastoral at that park (Leftwich?) with the falls where they took Lydia and her recently imported German girlfriend upon whom Jim has been rolling his eyes. After an exhausting afternoon pursuing the girls from craig to craig, they drove home —— Jim and Caio in the front seat —— while the girls made love in the back seat.

I got some Kitty Litter and Susie loves it. She pees and pees.

Best love
Louise

To tell the truth, at this point I was scared stiff of James Card. His was a violent temper. The "headaches" were an excuse to vamoose. If I returned to Rochester, it would be to visit Louise and I stayed at the Treadway Inn, hoping not to encounter Jim Card.

I would miss a lot being with his marvelous dear wife and the enchanting girls. They were sunlight and warmth to his cold draft from doomsday.

I believe Jim wished to run his life in those days as if he were at the Kit Kat Klub in 1928 Berlin. His shenanigans should be left to the imagination.

However let me say he was fiercely jealous of the relationship between Louise and myself. He felt he had invented her. At least re-invented her. And would share none of her with a whippersnapper from Ohio.

The next letter is from *Lillian Gish* to Louise, who copied it and sent it to me. Since I had a hand in the Garbo and Gish piece in *Sight and Sound*, she thought to share it.

LILLIAN GISH
June 9 1959

Dear Louise Brooks:

I cannot sail for Italy without sending you a note of thanks, admiration and wonder! First my gratitude—then my pride that a woman of our profession had so fine a writing talent—then amazement that you could delve so long and deep as to learn so much of the tactics of the company and people you write about. My own family did not know of many of the things in your article.

I hope you will continue to write as you have a rare gift that ought to be used. I had hoped to meet you. Perhaps I may have that pleasure when I return, as my sister and I are sailing for a motor trip through Jugoslavia, Bulgaria and maybe Russia.

May your summer be happy. Deepest thanks.

Lillian Gish

I read once—don't know if it's so—that Miss Gish had a Rolls Royce at her disposal. Somewhere the sisters had motor trouble. The Rolls Royce people obligingly flew a repair man from England to fix it.

Now Miss Gish's hope would quickly come true. And the following year, 1960, in a series "The Movie Star" at the Hebrew Y on Lexington Avenue, Louise made a charming impromptu speech after *Prix de Beauté* got screened.

That noon we lunched at Miss Gish's elegant flat. A highlight of my life! What the two said upon meeting I didn't hear, for I lingered in the tiny vestibule as they embraced and chatted.

At the dining table I recall Miss Gish mentioning John Huston's *The Unforgiven* (poor title) in which Lillian was to portray Audrey Hepburn's mother. Louise pouted.

For more about this two-star luncheon, see my *Through A Lens Darkly*.

Years pass. At the Gish Film Theater on the campus of Bowling Green State University, Miss Gish didn't recall the event. I had the notion she made another judgment about L.B.'s essay and did not care to discuss it.

Might be the way Miss Gish gazed at me.

She said in an odd tone, "You must be thinking of my sister Dorothy!"

Saturday June 27 1959
2155 East Avenue
Rochester 10 NY

Dear Junior

You bad boy. TOILET PAPER! Alice Morris said exactly what I said, only in a thousand less words. And she is right. If you had planted the plot in the beginning, I wouldn't have been pulled up at its revelation and had to get my interest back all over with your development. But anyhow, Jan, I don't think you should work over old material. It's like re-cooking a batch of sugared fudge. It takes hours and hours and never does come out right.

And I have seen a lot of rejection slips, but never one saying "beautifully written."

Now the thing you have to do is break down and write from a single viewpoint—yours. You are not Dickens, who had to be grown to full insight at the age of 25 (a Parliument reporter with 7 people to keep) or Goethe with his panoramic genius. You are much more like James Joyce who wrote true until he decided he was grown up. With your perfect technique, your lovely imagery, your infinite care, why can't you sit down and write a story out of the mind and soul of Jan Wahl? Posing for self-edification will get you nowhere unless you are willing to fall into the slave-writer group. Writing for other phonies.

In this day of "juvenile delinquency," what could throw more light, be of greater interest than your angle on sex, success and courage? Thousands of unreached kids and parents will say (reading Goodhousekeeping), "That's like us—that's our problem." It isn't the rape and murder that's killing our country. It's the imposition of FUCK, FUCK, FUCK, and success that ruins our youth and makes them think that truth, excellence, and work—no higher judge than other stupid men—is idiocy.

Watching Jim, I have learned more about sex than in any other way. In his grotesque way he shows the norm. But I will explain to myself.

Until I was 22 I treated sex as it should be treated. A few moments. Then I began to fail financially. Sex, I was taught, was the way back. I am no Zsa Zsa Gabor. The part of the whore fits me ill. But then it becomes a challenge. This man backs away! I will conquer him with my Asta Neilson! I was great, I thought. Men fell in love with me, men wanted to marry me—how would you like me as Mrs Roland Cocks, Guarentee Trust, Bronxville, NY?

Now I see the answer. Everytime Jim takes me to the Brighton some man, Jim says, Reddington or Issacs or Murphey, makes a pass at me. But for me it doesn't exist. I have recovered my youth. I am not vain with my fat old body and broken teeth. This man is looking for his own pleasure and triumph. In a word we screw ourselves with wanting to be SEXY AND SUCCESSFUL—wipe that out and as La Rouchfoucald said, "We would all be very good Catholics."

Love
Louise

This letter starts out lucidly enough. But grows wilder and wilder. Surefire sign the gin bottle was the muse.

Ah, Alice Morris.

The most interesting short stories were often found then on the pages of quality magazines such as *Harper's Bazaar* or *Mademoiselle*. The very, very young Truman Capote, the one who wrote lyrical poetic tales (collected in his haunting *Other Voices, Other Rooms*), began there. Alice Morris was the esteemed fiction editor at *Harper's Bazaar*.

Photo by Sorelle, Paris, 1930. Jan Wahl collection.

Although she didn't take my story in question, she bought one called "Heaven Bound." I got paid $300. Last time in Copenhagen I had seen a large Picasso woodcut from 1905, "Buste de Jeune Femme," at Erling Hagfeldt gallery on Bredgade.

The price? $300. Hooray, he still had it.

A few years later, I lived on crumbs in a gloomy Brooklyn Heights basement. A well-known dealer gave me the $300. I was so broke I took it. A week after, I met somebody from Harvard U.'s Fogg, who told me the dealer was asking fifty thousand.

Art and commerce. I'll never understand the disparity.

Monday — June 29 — 1959

Jan- this unmailed letter - eliptical and silly - has just enough truth to be passed by the *Brooks Board* of Review in favor of the better letter — (Dick Griffith got his start in the National Board of Review, Jim says.)

Two hours ago I was ready to scream in this murder=making heat as I did as a child in Kansas. Now, with 3 snorts of gin in my Belly, I care less. I put a clear dust ruffle on the bed where Miss Suzy Cat stretched herself for an afternoon nap. I feel at peace. No wonder Fr Egan snorted at my complaints against the smelly people at Mass. Cleanliness is not next to Godliness. It is a substitute - Just the same, it takes a lot of Gin and Toilet Water to overcome bad smells - other people's - My own I can't escape - a different stink in every Shire and County. You, like Greta, are among the Unstinkables - George Pratt told me that in London Greta said she disliked it most because the people were so dirty. But that is no reason for Wedlock, Jan.

And you want so terribly to Work - to have been of some use when you were here - even to help me wash dishes. I know your fear - in the first month working as a salesgirl at

Saks in 1946, I trembled before every customer - after 35 years of perfect equinimity at my job of dancing or acting -

And your unhappiness - Youth, beauty, talent, they mean nothing -

In 1933 the biggest boxoffice star was a viscious old stock-type symbol of the triumph of license called Marie Dressler. An audience which could not return to the unpunished selfishness of childhood, which was experiencing the delusion of sex, the danger of brutality and murder, the flatness of material success, was given the promise of the triumph by time - old age - filthy, greed, gluttony, cruelty - Unpunished -

Ask anyone today - Whom do they love - Elizabeth or Victoria?

Thursday July 2 1959———my letter gets sillier but now I shall send it—you'll get a bit of love out of it, anyhow. I had asked George Pratt and Arthur to lunch today and then Jim said he didn't want to have any more "personal relations" with them. This was a cover for his inner discontent with himself. Like house hunting and car shopping. A moment of exultation and years of misery with debt. "And what difference do these things make," I said. "You and your wife remain the same, 'shining alike in Palace or Privy.'" Now, he has done a little bookkeeping and decided to do LECTURES. And he can do marvelously at them. One sure fire lecture which he can compose out of all his tested performances. And it will make him so happy! Ham, ham, all of us. And Jimmie can make an audience laugh on lines that would get me rotten tomatoes. (I'm baking beans today. Remind me when it's 3:30) A good thing is that Jim goes to Vancouver the 2nd of August for their Festival for 2 weeks then to Sweden in September for FIAF. He plays lazy but he is a man of terrible energy turned inside out.

Suzy has just come in screaming from the bedroom with a bad dream. You seem to be cat—she is typing expert. But she is suffering from diarrhea because of her diet of raw kidney and canned milk. When I discipline her with decent diet—fish, Pussinboots, she starves. Yes, I spend a good deal of time looking across the street at the ruin. And sometimes the noise and dirt are terrible. But deep down the sorrow is age. Seeing my past come to nothing. Now I understand why people go to Europe, anywhere, unknown, unknowing, to die without the scars of the past.

July 8 1959 Wednesday. Seven letters wait answering and I go rambling on to you. But I have just finished St Teresa of Avila in THE EAGLE AND THE DOVE—the only book out of thousands given me that I wanted. What a great Saint——all that I reverence in a person. When Fr Egan gave me St Therese's name for my confirmation I put up a big beef, losing the argument for lack of knowledge. Later I read her and most of what has been written about her and, as usual, my intuitive knowledge was correct. She was so vain, and almost mean in choosing her "little way" to avoid the necessity of competing with the Great Teresa • And so sexy, in love with her favther, then with Our Lord. While, after drifting a bit at 16 towards Lesbos, St Teresa was forever freed of this destroying attachment. How shocked was Lotte in Paris with my contempt for the glories of sex.

The joy of reading again is immense! Two things decided me. Watching TV with squirms and cursing. And the consciousness that I have lost hundreds of words from my vocabulary and thousands of inspiring thoughts since I stopped reading (except for work and Scripture) in 1955. Sackville-West is not at the zenith but she is a model of excellence. Having read only half of St Teresa's autobiog-

raphy, I cannot test her there. Reading St. Therese, however, will give me a chance to analize her method—far
better, I think, than Lytton Strachey's—and put it to use in
my writing. Except for that magnificent English superiority
which deplores Spain and patronizes God. Thank Him that
my prayers were answered and the Holy Ghost took out
the criticisms of Lillian Gish in my article. 50 volumes of
Rushkin from 24 years to 70 had pointed the way. The
nasty things he wrote about Whistler, etc, that marred his
work, stopped and his writing grew true. For, isn't it the
truth that everything ugly we say of others turns out to be
mostly false, while the good turns out to be mostly true?

I will gobble up the St Therese essay and then I want
to read the Frank Sheed translation of The Confessions of
St Augustin. That I cannot read Latin, Greek, Italian, French,
German and Spanish makes me very sad. In English, I bow
to no one. At 18 when my FOLLIES dressing room shared
with Dorothy Knapp on top of the New Amsterdam Theatre
was the meeting place for those literary dilletantes Walter
Wanger, Henry Mankowitz, Michael Arlen and Gilbert Miller
who came to watch Dorothy bedeck and unbedeck herself
in front of a peerless glass, I learned the paucity of their love
and appreciation of literature. Mr. Ziegfeld had not banished
them from the stage door before I read all the Russians
they brought me and found that they had read only what can
be seen on a well waxed walnut book shelf. If only my
progress toward sanctity were as sure!

Dear little creature—I bought a transistor and I am
listening to lieder from Toronto. And I have Suzy, approving
of reading in the sitting room when she can sit on my lap –
hating TV.

But you must think of yourself. Think of every sexual
incident. What did it add? After 40 years experience I find
only that people come together to attempt or sometimes

achieve a triumph over another, "a thrill." A moment for a man involving babies, marriage, disease. For a woman—worse. What Sackville-West did not quote from St. Teresa (for like all the Bloomsbury Group).

Darling, I got up here to do the wash in the bathtub and forgot. Come down in September. You can rent a room here for little. We can make George (with his beard like a cunt and how he would hate the allusion) show us films. "Make" is not the word. We can all be very happy.

Louise

This is a lovely, rich letter—one to cherish, with a number of insights into her desire to remain Catholic. Three slugs of gin was just the right dose. The first part (June 29) is hand-written; July 2 and 8 are typed.

Greta was my Danish girlfriend.

Richard Griffith was the current head of the film department at MoMA.

George Pratt was Jim's highly-valued assistant, although he played games with him as he did with everyone else. George compiled a thick book, *Spellbound In Darkness*, that must be a classic for its title alone. I love great titles.

Arthur was a special friend. Somehow, for all Jim's rhapsodic obsession with Berlin of the Twenties, gay folk gave him the willies. When a number of magnificent, tastefully nude portraits of Ramon Novarro by Karl Struss vanished from Eastman House archives, Jim knew at once where they went.

FIAF = The International Federation of Film Archives. At first Jim Card was suspicious of it; however, after befriending Ernest Lindgren of the BFI and Henri Langois, he formed an alliance with them against MoMA's stubborn, dictatorial Film Library witch, Iris Barry.

Once (it was my first trip to the Museum of Modern Art) Iris Barry leaned out from the projection booth during a showing of E. A. Dupont's silent German classic VARIETY to shout: "*Look*! Lya da Putti has *dirty feet*!" I decided the lady might be a bit cuckoo.

I was told by Jim she ended up on a chicken farm in the South of France. I hope he didn't help put her there.

Friday 13 November 1959
2155 East Avenue
Rochester 10 NY

Dear Jan

That is a beautiful line in FLYING FISH—"I stand at the beginning and cannot remember the way." But I do not understand A NUN'S AFTERNOON OFF. The new school of writing baffles me. Like the Pre-Raphaelites of the 19th Century—or please pass the laudanum. One has to read and read and learn. As it is, I am blind. I grew up on the 19th century and gave up with ULYSSES. You will need an Ezra Pound to state your case. (I have not read ORLANDO.)

Jim says that Dartmouth has asked him to come and lecture with LULU. Have you a connection there too? Lillian Gish wrote yesterday asking me to lunch. But all my old fears have come back with a terrible column written about me here by Henry Clune arranged by Jim. Clune came loaded with gossip. Where did he get it? My appearance and the crucifix finished me. "Come on, everyone knows Card wrote that article. What about him? How do you live? You were never anything in pictures. Tell me about the men you knew," with a nudge, "I won't write anything." This is the first time I have ever been abused in print. And by a stranger. There is something deep and ugly here. To invent that playboy pop in the mouth.

Jim has not called or been around for two weeks except to bang the phone in my ear twice and to fly in "for some books" to see how the land lay. Tomorrow is my birthday and he hates giving presents.

In fact, more and more, he hates giving anything to anybody. When I first knew him 4 years ago there were still soft spots—now he has walled up a 13 year old boy forever behind the last heavy stone of abandonment. The day of the Clune piece, I noted, "How desperately sad he grows—clutching at the tiniest gnat reason to love himself."

Part, and the most dangerous part, of his delusion is that he is a lot smarter than he is and he takes down everybody else to match. In Stockholm Henri got in a hassle with FIAF and Jim "took his side." I knew some money Henri wanted to give Jim to give me had something to do with Jim's spending only 5 hours in Paris, but that he was more scared came out when he told me about a big article about Henri in the Sunday NY Times, Nov. 1. "We were very clever to get in on the ground floor—And my defending him in Stockholm." Until then I didn't dream that he could underrate Henri's wit and intelligence. Brusendorff has gone into the theatre business.

"Racing exaltation, despair." How well I know them. If only I were a greater person, less sinful, able to love—but I am only an occasional audience. In proud moments he boasts of all he denies in fear with bitching anger. More and more I make him angry.

He will begin to hate the grand expensive house when he finds it eating up all the money he likes to spend on himself. Polishing Goebels' 1936 Mercedes, which he bought from a man at Kodak, will lose its delight. He will grow angrier and angrier and turn his attention to Beaumont who is to go to FIAF next year instead of Jim.

And Beaumont is not the General. He knows a great deal about movies. He could replace Jim very easily. And when Jim said the other day, "I give Beaumont another year and a half," I begged him again to remember that Beaumont has many reasons not to love him. Beaumont is the Director, close to Kodak, and far from a fool. And he certainly has not forgotten the time Jim went to the General with a story of Beaumont and the rest plotting against the General.

Poor Jan, that you must listen to all my gloom and forbodings. And how miserably I have failed, wanting to

Jan Wahl at University of Michigan. Photo by Ray Bossert.

help, wanting to see Jim turn the whole of his being to the joy of making Eastman House the finest archive...

A FEARFUL SINNER - Louise

"Flying Fish" must have been a poem I had sent to Louise. Now long lost. A Copenhagen landlady, Oda Isbrand, the Greenland painter, once while I was absent cut up most of my poetry (typed out on onion skin paper) into neat little squares for toilet paper.

I was sure (wrong!) that Louise would like my story "A Nun's Afternoon Off." I am still fond of its opening sentence: "She was a woman of the world, though not of *this* world."

Orlando, by Virginia Woolf, I thought Louise might enjoy reading; I mentioned I was sure it could make a terrific movie, if done right.

Henry Clune I assume wrote for a Rochester paper.

Ove Brusdendorff: see earlier letters.

Beaumont = Beaumont Newhall, Jim's nemesis at Eastman House, had been Curator of Photography and then was appointed Director. The museum's first Director had been General Oscar Solbert. The General in theory drowned himself in his bathtub on the top floor. However, as Louise reported, he was still wearing his watch.

1960

Friday February 5 1960
2155 East Avenue
Rochester 10 NY

Dear Sulkyshoes

Thinking that you would write me so that I would know whether you were here or there, I have not written you to thank you for the exquisite medal and chain.

New York was so complicated. Butch went into that badly contrived hotel-room sequence to compensate for what she felt to be a bit part. Johnnes was furious about not being allowed to play a fascinating dictator of the theatre.

Peggy Fears was indignant at the sight of Jane Kent.

Glennon was indignant at the sight of "that lad."

You were concerned because of Nat Perlow who writes: "make it very anecdotal and write about all the movie great/??/?? who crossed your path with a favor of intimacy…But don't overlook the colorful personalities themselves; their secrets,…" Nat is not for me.

When you were screaming about Macmillan I had no time to tell you that Painter had asked for something after she read my little piece about Pabst in *Image.* At the time I had no idea of writing. The Brooks-Card of Joan Crawford was sent in to Painter to convince Jim that he was a fine writer who should bear down on his work. (And his Pickford article in the new *Image* is sharp, particular, fresh—good.)

Anyhow, Junior, in my 53 years, with my endless reading I have also noted endlessly the publisher. Macmillan is for Arthur Knight.

And you, dear glum boy. In New York, you had written a play and no one played his part. All of us dropped your script.

Johnnes never wrote me who to thank for the flowers, although Jimmie got a more grateful letter from Vogal. And Jim had a fine time with Jane Kent whom I arranged for him to meet—or did I tell you?

Best Love
Louise

(Letters missing from July to February.)

I had seen "Once Upon a Mattress," the musical farce. While my goal was to catch Buster Keaton as the king, it was Carol Burnett as the princess (who slept on the pea) who caught my eye.

I wrote Louise here was a star in the making. My former roommate at Cornell, Mark Perrier, thought the same. He used her in a TV commercial as a chorus girl who kicked in the wrong direction. "Who could be funnier than Buster Keaton?" grumbled Brooks.

After the showing of PRIX DE BEAUTÉ at the Hebrew "Y," my head was awhirl. The luncheon Chez Gish momentarily ebbed away.

In this epistle, February 5, Louise packs in some bit players, namely:

Peggy Fears had been a showgirl with Louise (the Follies and Scandals) and now was an extremely rich woman who practically owned Fire

Island. Her girlfriend, "Miss Fairweather," a regular on Tallulah Bankhead's Sunday afternoon radio program, was the one at Glennon's who threw up on her chinchilla wrap.

Why Jimmie Glennon objected to my presence, I don't know.

Jane Kent was a notorious figure from Louise's later years in the City. Louise likened her to the demi-mondaine portrayed by Joan Crawford in *Grand Hotel*.

Charlotte Painter, the editor at Macmillan who optioned my novel, also had an interest in a possible book by Louise.

Amos Vogel was head of Cinema 16.

Scott Schutte collection.

PRIX DE BEAUTÉ and escorting Louise around, plus futile attempts to keep her in shape (away from temptation), drained my energy.

Afterwards at Glennon's and at the hotel room packed with denizens of her past life and its messiness, I was at wit's end. A lesbian named Butch tried to start a fight. I didn't want to be trapped in scenes beyond my understanding.

I fled Hotel Lexington in confusion.

Sunday – 6:25 a.m. – Feb – 28 – '60

Junior – I am dashing this off to mail toward Mass –
Thank you for the lovely Valentine Chocolates –
I am getting my teeth fixed – caps – the works –
Feel so happy – 7 years hold out – misery – Can't chew so
I am losing Weight too –

Random House nibbling at book – Working hard on
my film lists and correct Biographies – the book is laid out
– 10 dames and me ——

> Write me
> Love
> Brookstein

Portrait by Steichen, Hollywood, 1928. Jan Wahl collection.

Brief. But merry.

Now *Thirteen Women in Films* was Ten. Or would it be Eleven if we count Louise?

Already she had attempted some stories and autobiographical *Naked on My Goat* of which I had a chance to peek at one chapter, Six: WHO IS THE EXOTIC BLACK ORCHID, before she abandoned it. Louise was tough on her writing. Into the wastebasket.

Actually, *Naked* is not autobiography, it's a novel. The heroine, a chorus girl, Mary Porter, gets her chance in a revue like George White's Scandals to do a specialty number during a Chinese act.

Mary has eight bars of music exactly to do thirty-two little Chinese steps to knock out the audience just as Louise had done in the 1925 Summer "Follies" against competition from headliners Will Rogers, W. C. Fields, comedienne Ray Dooley, singer Vivienne Segal. According to the July 8 *New York Evening World*, Louise's dance was a show-stopper.

Like Brooks, Mary Porter reads the Russians and listens to highbrow music. The other girls think Ravel and Debussy is a French bicycle set.

Naked's style is vintage Twenties, the inspiration not Scott Fitzgerald but lighthearted Anita Loose.

In 1980 Loos became Louise's biggest fan, declaring, "Louise Brooks became the greatest actress in the history of moving pictures." Well. Perhaps over the top.

Louise and I were heading toward the same goal. Stories and articles, fine and dandy. A book, however, is more substantial. You hold it in your hands.

Monday March 28 1960
2155 East Avenue
Rochester 10 NY

Jimmie says that a letter he sent to Toledo was forwarded to your New York address and returned. However, I shall send this on because Jim is existing in the expedience of Pride. He has reached a point of circling confusion; unable to find his way back to the do-nothing pleasure in his daydream; without yet the will and the faith and the muscles of work it takes to destroy the image of himself copied from other copies – for you can't copy what is great (the living personality) in a person. What did the Carmelite nun say – "We do not seem worth anything special to God until we look at ourselves as in a mirror, looking, looking, looking until we see what has never been seen before, what could not be copied or invented because until we give it reality in one unique and perfect way of loving and serving God, it does not exist." I think at once of Helen Keller.

Yes. I think JACKAL, WOLF, AND FOX is as good a short story as I have ever read. Technically perfect in form and cutting, the building of suspense. My test of the written word is the film that develops in my mind following along with the script. Along with the thoughts and feelings evoked by my own experience. With this story every frame is sharp and clear. You did not invent crazy people I could not see and try to put me down with deeds and words I could not understand. You gave me people and situations which I could fill with life.

The greatest scene is when you find her sleeping among her dogs. The greatest moment is when Blanche is hugging her dog and shrinking into the shadow – shrinking from the evil which fear and rejection will make her do.

I have just heard of Mailer's book, ADVERTISING MYSELF. How pitiful.

You are nothing in your story, but for the first time in your writing, I see you. I don't like what you are. And when you write your way to your giving of your inimitable gift to the world you won't have to sic your dogs on us – we will love you for "enlarging our soul." For being an adorable person.

ST JOHN OF THE CROSS "…To arrive at that which one ignores, one must follow the road where one ignores. To arrive at that which one has not, one must follow the road where one has not. To arrive at that which one is not, one must follow the road where one is not. To obtain the All, one must abandon all. And when you come to possess the All, hold it without wanting anything at all."

You already possess the gift of giving gifts – not to show off or giving something we ought to like because you like it. Everything you have ever given me has been right for me. The magazine had a marvelous piece on Murnau which I sent to Lotte. The Mal St. Clair article is most useful to me. Yes, that is my sister. And I like reading these magazines which I would never see but for you. I must dip into Griffin on Orwell language. How do these poems read set up as ordinary prose? birdswill, twittering, glittering, look at me, I'm special, special, special.

Another two weeks and I shall have my clean, smiling mouth full of $1,500 teeth. If I don't die of fur balls in the meantime. Suzy is "Blanching" me.

Come to Rochester if you can. I would love to see Martha's spring concert in New York but I've got 2½ years to pay on my teeth.

Love Louise

Martha = Martha Graham, a fellow classmate of hers in the early Twenties with the Denishawn (Ruth St. Denis and Ted Shawn) Dancers.

Bingo. By gum, Louise approved of my story! Like others I was writing, I wrote from a child's perspective. A child attempting to grasp the unfathomable adult world. In my twenties I was still trying to grasp it.

I stayed in New York. Temporarily. Talk about a fish out of water! Yet I fell in with a heavy-hitting art crowd including Robert Barnes, Phillip Pearlstein, Jim Dine, Marcel Duchamp, Leon Golub, Edward Hopper.

Dine offered me one of his flag paintings at $300 one day. ($300 was a popular sum in those days.) Why would I want a crummy American flag depiction when I could have a finished tiny elegant pen & ink by Aubrey Beardsley. Or for $75 a Walter Crane watercolor The Cow Jumped Over the Moon?

I was dining on air sandwiches yet made one glorious investment. After I had stared at, over the bar at Glennon's, the framed page of *Vanity Fair* with Edward Steichen's August 1928 portrait of Louise, I rushed to MoMA and told Capt. Steichen's assistant Grace Mayer I wanted to order a print pronto.

Steichen replied I was the very first person in all the years to ask. He added that shot, now a famous one, was the third exposure he took.

Next off to Max Granick's on West 67th Street where, in the work room, I glimpsed frame pixies stepping on stockinged feet over a set of Picasso color lithographs strewn on the floor.

What a town.

2155 East Avenue
Rochester 10 NY
Thursday September 22 1960

Dear Jan

I am not going to New York. Not tomorrow at any rate. In the end, unless I must, I never go anyplace unless I am dragged by the hair. I love being there, but I hate going there.

Jim's "revenge" is sure but never predictable. After nothing but snarls since I threw Kent out ot town, he called me full of love and misunderstanding from New York Tuesday night leading up to telling me that he was taking a 6'2" lesbian whore whom he had met at the Les-Pan joint, PATSY'S, to Europe on the Queen Elizabeth.

Scott Schutte collection.

Not believing because it would cost about $3,000 and where would he get it? I checked with George who had been out with them and he did believe it. Then I called him back and screamed. That was what he wanted. Waiting for George to tell me, George didn't and Jim had to tip his mit by calling me himself. That is what inflames me. Being neither wife nor mistress, how he spends his time or money has not concerned me for a long time. But I am concerned with his job and his keeping it (and when he wants money, look out) because, first after I knew the score, my guilt and my desire to make reparation was great (Dear girl, his wife forgave me long ago); then there is so much good in Jim; and then if he hangs himself with the rope of debt and scandal which is dangling for him (for Kodak has a spy system which is its main strength – genius can count on itself – office holders not), the Communists will control Eastman House.

This morning from Winick, who cares less for me than a supermarket cashier, I got another letter fixing me for a grant from (now) the Bollingen Foundation. He is coming here. Why should he care? And when you can't answer that question (usually filling it in with your charm,) you are being taken.

In a world full of words I have failed. George brought me this Yeats poem...."Now all the truth is out, Be secret and take defeat From any brazen throat, For how can you compete, Being honour bred, with one Who, were it proved he lies, Were neither shamed in his own Nor in his neighbours' eyes? Bred to a harder thing than Triumph, turn away And like a laughing string Whereon mad fingers play Amid a place of stone, Be secret and exult, Because of all things known That is most difficult."

Louise

The name *Winick* escapes me.

It was a turbulent season. I dropped out of the loop.

My Brooks-Card loop.

Because my novel was optioned by Macmillan, someone said I should get "writer's privilege" at Princeton. I was put up in a creaky frame two-story house from 1800 on the main street. The last occupants were poet Allen Tate and his wife, author Caroline Gordon.

J. Robert Oppenheimer rolled by in his Silver Ghost, a shiny Rolls Royce. I attended a puppet show performed by critic Dwight MacDonald and novelist Mary McCarthy (*The Group).*

At a party, H. T. Lowe-Porter, otherwise faithful translator of Thomas Mann, boasted she turned down his last novel, *The Black Swan,* since "it is a filthy book" (a mid-life German woman, dying of cancer, falls in love with a young G. I.).

Philip Roth, another Princeton resident, and I were both at the starting gate. Though Little, Brown had lately rejected *Dancing on the Shore* in a five-page letter. The upshot, decided the editor: "It was like opening a box of beautiful ribbons."

On a trip to the Big Apple (luxury, train from Princeton), I was to lunch with my agent Candida Donadio and Alfred Knopf, publisher of my beloved Willa Cather. The venerable gent tested me.

"Let the young man order the wine."

Bewildered, I begged off. I had no expertise with the grape. "We can't publish him!" he snorted and promptly left the table.

At Princeton, the Tates, converts to The Church, saw me "near the door." Mrs. Tate felt I was a prime candidate. She delivered me, at the local Carmelite establishment on a sultry summer afternoon, to the top nun.

This awesome personage stood at a barred window—a mastiff lay by her feet. Despite August heat, she seemed knee-deep in roses. She sighed.

"Sometimes we feel sorry for those of you out in the world." Yes indeed.

Dinner at the Tates was singular: they ate in separate rooms. The soup course was with Caroline, the short-story writer and cook; followed by a main course in the living-room with Allen, the poet. The dessert course was back again in the kitchen with the mistress of the house; it ended by having coffee with him.

Although I had shown no inclination to join the Faith to which they both converted, Mrs. Tate—Caroline Gordon—asked if I wished to join them, to become their "new Hart Crane."

For Hart Crane, the American poet who penned the epic "The Bridge," lived with them once, sharing a farmhouse. At one point none of the three were speaking to one another. To communicate, they slipped notes under the door. I was flattered that I was chosen to be the "new Hart Crane," but more than that was appalled. I simply put on a smile and stammered, "No thanks."

Not for me.

The house I was in was haunted. I refuse to believe, I would tell myself. In the middle of night a long iron bolt got pulled back noisily and I woke up. Enough time elapsed for "it" slowly to cross the room. The bolt on the door opposite, leading to a closed-in porch, slid back. Eeek.

This happened more than once. I ran to the Tates. They revealed a priest had exorcised the place. Without success. Allen and Caroline suggested I bring in a subhuman intelligence, cat or dog, to cancel "my" poltergeist.

Before I was able to banish any ghost, someone I knew broke in—slit his wrists—hit me with a heavy object—and raped me.

To say I was ill after that would be an understatement.

I skedaddled to Toledo.
With no explanation to Louise.

Wednesday October 26 1960
2155 East Avenue
Rochester 10 NY

Dear Jan

I cannot accept your lovely Pavlova only to put it away
in the WAHL envelope. You must keep your treasures for the
day when you will have a place of your own in which to display
them. But thanks for the beautiful mark of affection.

Now Jan, in spite of getting so irritated, bored and
displeased with you that I scream, I love you at the same
time for your underlying sense, subtlety and integrity. Jim,
soon or later, tells everything he knows, either out of mind or
mindless malice, or the necessity to puke up his guilt. He
has never been able to repeat anything said between you
and me. After my return from New York last January he told
one of these crude liar's lies attempting to catch me in a lie.
One afternoon in the theatre, he said that he had a letter
from you implying that you had spent the night with me in
New York. I said, "Well, go upstairs and get it — show it to
me." And that was the end of it.

You also have the ingredient as necessary to success as breath of life – toughness. You do not allow anyone
to destroy your self-esteem or your faith in your art. Selling
writing and selling acting are exactly the same in this: Most
buyers know nothing of either art and they are equally jealous of what they, who can do nothing, call the writer's gift
and the actor's intuition. As long as you are young and
pretty and willing to be used and abused, they will lead your
hope and feed your vanity while they destroy your vision.

If you go about your work in purity, without regard
for sex, money or fame – for these are the traps of the
exploiters, one day somebody will come to you asking

nothing more than the right to publish your work. It will be so easy that past struggles will look silly. But art can not be sold. It must be found. However you must be working with all your heart. What the gamblers who are geniuses in human nature call "being in action." In Hollywood, I used to watch them casing the night clubs and restaurants night after night without finding a sucker, and then when they were down to a sawbuck, Lasky or Sam Goldwyn would come to *them* looking for a game of bridge or poker.

If you want success you must get yourself a job in a publishing house or on a magazine. After a time they will publish your work because it will be just like theirs.

As for your troubles with Jim, you must work them out for yourself. I have learned that it is bad to give or take advice on how to handle another person. Jim's desires and fears in relation to you are totally different from his conflict with me. And on my part, as I told him, Sept. 20, I AM FINISHED. If I see him and can put in a plug for you, certainly I will. But I have seen him only once (when he came last week to bring Lotte's Japanese book) since August 14. After 5 years of having subjected myself to his jerking malice and degradation and the confusion of a cesspool of lies, it is like diving into a clean cool pool to be free of him …

(In this letter, Louise unleashes much anger about a dive in New York known as Patsy's – I am sparing you the details. – J.W.)

… It happens every night in traps around such gin mills to the Smart, Special people. I know. I have been through it. But a man who believes that whores LOVE him and degenerates RESPECT him will not believe what I tell him.

[DELETION]

For the rest, I tell Jim nothing – AND DON'T YOU; I pray to God that he will not come here drunk. And that he will accept a friendly relationship with me for our mutual good. In looking back, however, I cannot name a single good he has ever done me without the object of either explicating me or injuring me. But I can't go away – I have not the money.

Forgive me for writing all this, but remember that I am always alone, and it clears my mind to write you.

Love

Louise

A TROUBLED letter. Needed editing.

Pavlova = Anna Pavlova, the Russian ballet dancer famous for her "The Dying Swan," which Doug Fairbanks' cameraman Arthur Edeson miraculously filmed in 1924 on the set of *The Thief of Bagdad*. Louise returned my original photo which, decades later, I gave to a young ballerina who cherished it.

Card and Brooks were quits. She was residing down the street from George Eastman House. Convenient and not so convenient.

Notice Mr. Card isn't Jimmie anymore. This Jim is a bad dream—the Jim who saw me wrongly as a threat.

Gleefully, he had enjoyed pulling strings. George Pratt was of a certain kind of bent, a handsome fellow, eager and helpful. Jim hired a gorgeous damsel as a secretary and both young people of necessity, in the office, throughout the day, worked elbow to elbow.

The lady was of a different persuasion. She needed constant affection, if you get my drift, from a man. Nearly tore her tresses out in agony when George failed to succumb. This did not have a happy ending.

When I think of Jim Card, I prefer to think on the visits when I was a teenager and everything felt new, the small and large generosities, the coziness of cramped Marion Street, the heady scent from Kodascope prints in the fruit cellar, the private 16mm viewings of Max Linder's *Seven Years' Bad Luck*, on the same night Ernst Lubitsch's *Sumurun* with flamboyant

Pola Negri and Lubitsch himself as the Hunchback and, in between, tasty snacks in the kitchen and homemade ice cream sodas.

And at Eastman House with its 1001 Nights wonders, special 35mm showings for me alone of *A Kiss for Cinderella* with irresistible Betty Bronson in a genuine tinted nitrate and the eerie mystery of Frank Wysbar's dark fable *Ferryman Maria* with lovely, doomed Sybille Schmitz, and it didn't matter that I didn't know German: there was hardly any dialogue.

How honored I was to bring my precious 16mm print of Pabst's *L'Atlantide* with regal, glamorous Brigitte Helm who had played the mystical Maria and the robot woman in *Metropolis*. In the Pabst fantasy she was the enchantress Antinéa who lured Foreign Legionaires to their deaths in the Sahara.

All this before that other enchantress—sad, exhilarating and musical-voiced Louise Brooks.

After Louise, entering Rochester was skating on slippery ice. My solid support was from his wife and from her unwavering faith and goodness and sense of humor.

(handwritten)

Dec . 1 . 1960
2155 East Avenue
Rochester . 10 . 1960

Jan – Enclosed your letters and ORDET which I think very beautiful with exquisitely written descriptive passages. How I wish I could do as well for Chaplin in *The Word & Movement in Films*. I do not see Jim anymore but I called him about your trouble and he said your films were mailed back to you book rate and he will return the Framed Dreyers. He is growing more evil every day and boasts of it. If I told you what he said about you! But I am afraid you would tell him and I am scared to death that he will get drunk and come here and tear me apart. He is very angry because I have finished with him. But have no more to do with that evil man, Jan, or Eastman House.

And don't ask George to do anything – He dares not make a move without Jim – it has taken great courage for him to be my friend in the face of Jim's animosity – Do your writing, dear boy, grown up writing – Not like that enfantile shit, shit, shit – *At the Crossing* –

Ted Shawn and Martha Graham tango, 1922. Jan Wahl collection.

Thanks for the picture of Martha and Ted – it's a tango but I don't remember the name – They almost never did it after 1923 –

Your anger has made you a little silly – God, how I understand – Just to talk on the phone sets me in a rage – But it absolutely destroys the mind – So cut him out of your life – perhaps we can see each other and talk –

Love
Louise

Louise put a *P.S.* atop the Dec. 1 letter:

Yes, Ted wants me to
read "1001" if you
have it ——

"1001 refers to his autobiography. Ted = Ted Shawn.

Ordet? I was working on the book about Carl Theodor Dreyer and may have sent her my piece from the Danish magazine *Kosmorama*.

As always, she considered silent film acting as a ballet and no better examples can be found than in Keaton or Chaplin. She adored them both.

My story "At the Crossing" was not a hit; she was in a foul mood.

No, Jim failed to return loaned film prints or original stills Dreyer had given me; happily Dreyer was able to replace some stills.

She liked the Ted Shawn-Martha Graham photo. I didn't read danger signs. Wait till you read Dec. 19th's letter.

As much as anything, the following incident demonstrates Jim "writing" real-life scenarios. A mind-bender.

On a whim, Jim, to get back at me, hired as secretary a Danish girl I was partial to. Let us call her Greta Olsen. He planned an elaborate set-up, and sent duplicate wires to a number of film distributors and the like in New York, Tom J. Brandon and John E. Allen among them.

Greta was to arrive on a Norwegian liner. Jim told the fellows his knock-out secretary was arriving. Would they meet her with candy and flowers at the pier. As a favor, escort her to Rochester.

All were enthusiastic. They owed Jim something.

Naturally he had to see how this unfolded with his own eyes, so he arrived early, and mentioned to reporters there to meet the ocean liner—did they know a Norwegian iceskating champion was aboard? So now a goodly passel of men were ready to greet her.

Poor Greta. What none knew, well, Jim did but had forgotten, is that Greta's sister was married to an American whose mother, Rose, lived at the Waldorf Towers. Rose had an opinion that all men potentially were white slavers. And she too would meet the boat to forewarn the unsuspecting Dane.

Boat docked, Jim lurked in the shadow, Greta was alarmed to be greeted loudly by men bearing flowers and candy and cameras. "White slavers!" screamed Rose, rushing to save the victim.

The girl was aghast. The film distributors looked at one another, each bearing expensive gifts. Rose grabbed Greta, whisking her away in the limo. His plot in tatters, Jim rushed out to take a taxi to follow to the Waldorf Towers, where he bribed his way up and banged on doors until he heard a voice calling for help. Rose was giving the white slaver lecture.

On the same flight to Rochester were booked a half dozen seats for a half dozen Greta Olsens.

Jim and Greta verified the story. It tickled Jim's fancy. Worried Greta.

I promise to continue this saga in the next installment.

2155 East Avenue
Rochester 10 NY
December 7 1960

Dear Jan

I won't go into your last letter than to say that when I called him about you it seemed to give him a new vicious approach to me. At the time I told him he should not write such nasty letters to you, especially mentioning Brandon and John Allen, because sometime he was going to come up against some one whom he could not bully and abuse. He was frightened then and asked, no, told me not to return his letter to you. I said I had to return the letter.

In return for this he called me last night at twelve thirty. He snarled and sneered and said that he was coming over to "lay it on the line." I told him that he must not come here drunk at night, that he could see me in the day time. Then he said he would cut me off from George and everything in Rochester. I lay awake in fear for a long time.......

[DELETION]

I called George this morning to tell him in case he was afraid to see me anymore.

Since he is the only living soul, as Jim knows, whom I see – the loss of his friendship would be sad.

Only fear moves him. Your letter to Beaumont. Your films restored.

[DELETION]

...And if only fear did not rob me of my senses.......

[DELETION]

This is my home. I love it. Does this man really think he can run me out of town because, no longer able to use me as a reflection of his evil, he wants to destroy me?

May God have mercy on me. For two years I have been asking reparation for my sin against marriage. He sinks deeper and deeper in vice and tries to make me the victim of his wickedness.

Pray for me.

And in God's name, if you love me, do not repeat anything, ANYTHING, I say...He can now invent a reason for the foulest action out of a 4 cent stamp. That is his most fearful insanity. He believes his lies. Screams

(*Unsigned*)

Card may have been her demon. One of many demons.

She described the brutality and showed me, at my next secret visit, badly bruised fingers. It hurt her to type—that did not stop her. I wept at her isolation.

She fretted over the $1500 fragile teeth.

The "good" connection lasted from late 1955 to 1958 after the return from Copenhagen, Paris and Barcelona.

Remember I told you of Greta Olsen's first day on these shores? Now for the last day in Rochester.

Immediately Greta and Louise became chums. This did not pass well in Jim's eyes. For one, he felt left out and suspected they might be intimate, too intimate.

It was a summer's eve. Lousie had arranged an artful repast for Greta and herself. They were leisurely supping when Jim burst in, expecting to find the two beauties in a compromising situation. He was disappointed.

Louise's TV was on the blink. Suddenly her repairman, a fine-looking Egyptian, coyly stuck his head against the window screen to inquire, "O. K. if I come in, honey?"

This was the limit. Jim picked up the wine bottle and did a bit of damage. Greta fled from Rochester that night. She came to Toledo looking for me.

I was up in Canada on the north shore of Lake Erie in Ontario with my good chum Keith Lampe. Keith and I soon would be cooking up an idea: students against war.

An exhausted Greta unburdened herself of the distressing exit from Rochester. To cheer her up, I had read that Sophie Tucker (Sophie Tucker—was she still alive?) was appearing at a supper club in Windsor.

"Sophie Tucker is important—let's go. We'll remember this forever!"

We arrived for the midnight performance. The waiter was displeased when we ordered only basic nibbles: olives, carrot strips and pickles at $25 a pop. At last, drum roll. And a spotlight shone on, yes, a hefty Sophie "The Last of the Red Hot Mamas" Tucker. Incredibly, she wore a glittery metallic astronaut's suit, to prove she was up-to-date.

The M.C. let us know "Sophie Tucker can sing anything. Just call out your request."

Someone from ringside called, "Sing one of the Beatles' songs!" Sophie's face went blank. What in hell was a beetle song?

"NO!" shouted a stooge from the rear of the club. "Sing 'One of These Days'!" In triumph she belted that one out. Of course it was her signature tune.

After this peculiar experience, we found a grim Sophie Tucker sitting at a card table in the lobby. You couldn't leave without passing her. In front of her was a pile of old 78 records. No long-plays for her. I decided a record was the perfect souvenir for Greta. Besides, no one else was buying.

If anybody represents the U.S.A., it's the Red Hot Mama.

A 78 was $25—same as the hors d'oeurves. She agreed to autograph and picked up, with a plump hand full of diamonds, the 78 lying on top. I was the only patron buying, so I thought I could pick.

"I'd like this one, please," I said and pushed her choice aside.

Sophie whacked me with her rings, ripping my skin. Drops of blood trickled over the tabletop. But, trouper that she was, Sophie Tucker signed "Some of These Days" without comment.

Greta returned to Denmark.

I heard she married a librarian from London.

2155 East Avenue
Rochester 10 NY
Monday December 19 1960

Jan

I am wild with rage that you make me write this letter. Why do you have to be hit over the head? Not because you are stupid. You are utterly selfish, unfeeling, unseeing. When I returned that Pavlova picture, you knew the score. I do not exchange or collect junk. I had to trot down in the rain to get an envelope and mail a photo back to you once before. (Of June and me.) Incidentally you still do not understand that the tango photo is Martha Graham – as an art collector you should be able to tell that, idiot. But then you know nothing of dance, or you would not have sent me that hideous picture of Miss Ruth.

To go to all the time and expense to send that picture!

For one hour I tore my broken hands apart unpacking it. And you will not get it back. I gave it away to keep from kicking it to pieces.

Haven't you learned your lesson from Jim? You send a lot of crap to people who neither ask for it nor want it. Then, when the favors you expect are not forthcoming you scream "stop, thief."

As I told you before, if you consider these things treasures, keep them.

Of course, you wouldn't notice, but there are never any photos around me. I keep them in envelopes for research. But I detest them exposed, staring at me.

And now, however mad I make you, perhaps you will stop this trick of shaking people down with unsolicited stuff that makes them furious. Naturally, I suppose you still have enough contact with the outside world to know that I do not mean myself – but people like Jim.

Louise

This one blew me away. No more did I pick perfect gifts. I had sent a signed photo of Ruth St. Denis, her teacher. I thought it a nice memento, maybe of use to illustrate an essay. Ha, no luck.

I could feel Louise's fury through the miles between us. Thunderous waves of displeasure shook the air. Better keep my distance. Perhaps, in retrospect, the photo may have resembled a death mask—although it was taken when Miss Ruth was a spry sixty. It failed to amuse or push the right button.

I made a point always of not asking favors. Not even to have her sign a photograph or to remind her that she said one day I was to have the Willy Pogany painting.

Two days later came the follow-up note written in bright red crayon.

I am sorry for
writing that
mean letter

Merry Xmas

Louise

Jan Wahl "art" photo by Marian Dorf, Ithaca.

1961

After the breakup with Card, more and more Louise turned toward the Church, saw the light and accepted the error of her ways.

Some letters, such as the one dated 18 January 1961, are weedy thickets. Hard to climb through. It was headed: "Oh, you miserable back-sliding boy."

Lots of quotes from Church figures, literary as well as those who were instructing her in Rochester (like Mother Digges). A favorite source was one Janet Stuart, Superior General of the Society of the Sacred Heart from 1911-14. Single-spaced quotes of such length they flew over the head of this lapsed Presbyterian.

I may have made a mistake in saying I had stuck in my mind a title, "How the Children Stopped the Wars." Did she think I dabbled in Catholic territory? I was borrowing from a supposed Children's Crusade of 1212. A shepherd boy, Stephen, followed by 30,000 children, set out from Vendome to capture Jerusalem. This was merely the seed from which my fable was to grow. The immediate spark was Viet Nam.

Louise could not resist the comment: "Hardly a subject to be caught in a butterfly net."

I resolved never to send her the finished text.

"You see," she wrote, "behind the glasses, you do have the eyes of purity. If you could have seen the super-cilious tilt of Langlois's and Card's big heads condemning

Willy Pogany. It is true, as far as I am concerned, that his painting was very close to the Midway, but in this swift sketch he has distilled all that is good in me. For 36 years I have looked after it. I knew Card to be a phoney, but Langlois's judgement made me mad."

She closed: "Now, don't sulk — write me everything you feel. Go to the Church and see what God says."

Love,
Louise

Was she implying I wore rose-tinted glasses?
I spent the next half year honing my fable.

Monday June 12 1961
2155 East Avenue
Rochester 10 NY

Jan

You darling for sending me the Martha Graham. And the Lady Chapel where I used to sit every day...

About your New York trip. What you need is just one person in a publishing house to fall in love with you or your work. Since, like me, you appeal to both sexes. It makes everything half as easy and twice as hard. It takes a cool head. Hard to get. Indifference. I didn't lose them till I ran out of money. But that doesn't mean being silent, sulky, and slew-footed. It means being busy, too busy to care.

Peggy Fears sent me the notice of the opening of her hotel, PINES YACHT CLUB, Fire Island. Now if you go to New York, go out there and talk to her. She never gave me a bum steer in my career. And she would understand you too. She has more connections than the Bell Telephone Company.

Funny switch on Paris. Langlois called me the night he left New York for Paris. He had holed in at the Wellington, gathered together the happy group and had a week of unconfined pleasure.

The night he left Rochester he stopped by to pick up a pound of walnut fudge and I showed him your photograph and suddenly a lot of things about Ove and Jim came clear to him.

Jim seems to be growing accustomed to my new face. About his TV show I wrote him a note telling him how handsome he looked but he shouldn't sit facing the camera with his legs spread...He answered. And then when Fr Cousineau was down at the Ascension, he took me to lunch at the Treadway with his dear guardian priest who has finally put the okay on me and Father said that he had driven back at the same time from Montreal with Jim who showed LULU and gave a wonderful lecture on me and Mr. Pabst. "That is how he is," I said, "when I said at dinner with Langois and Jim, 'I suppose you have burned all my films,' it was a sure way of saving them. But I do not love people who must be vilified to act well. And I do NOT forgive him!" Father laughed, thinking, "But you do." And when I showed him the Chaplin part of my script about Chaplin's imitation of a boy and a fear of social disease (wanting to see Father's reaction), until then, Father really believed that Jim did write my articles. Now, I would love to have Jim read my script but he will use all of my material and people will go on saying he wrote it. Otherwise, I would be delighted. But why else do I write? But I like to, would like to get established——if I am any good——first. N'est pew?

If I send it to you, will you *read* it, *critic* it, and RETURN it?

Lotte Eisner who will translate it for the Cinématheque Française Magazine, History of Film (French), IMAGE (?) writes...

"My dear you are grand. It is wonderful to be beautiful and intelligent. But you are more: You are wise. And what a lot you know." (Ten months work for *25* pages——ha!) "Wonderful what you write about Chaplin!!!"

But here is a plug for getting truth and fact straight, for in my first draft I had written as if Gordon Craig was dead. Lotte writes — "When I was with a friend in *Cannes* our dear Gordon Craig rang up my hotel to invite me to a most lovely lunch with this friend in St Paul de Vence. He is still interested in everything and a great character loving life and art at *85.*"

The finished essay which Lotti received simply quoted Craig.

And I think you will like what I wrote about Martha. A short quote...

"If genius is defined as a spirit presiding over the destiny of a person, then Martha has no peer. Coming late to dance at the age of twenty, she did not struggle hopelessly with ballet technique; she welded her tiny feet (deformed by too tiny shoes) into angry hoofs and kicked it to death. Spreading her legs, turning up her toes, she kneaded her body into the shapes of fantastic pretzels and set them on end in defiance of all the laws of balance.."

And now a strange experience in which you are innocently made a rival.

The first of April a letter forwarded from Eastman House, John de Lungo, English, London, saw LULU, fell in love with me. New experience for me. Answered. Because he obviously was no Art Fan, never heard of me. Sent me photo. Tall dark and handsome. I was intrigued. He said many of the things you wrote in your article about me which I did not believe when YOU said them. It was fun. I answered. Letters have poured in. I sent him old as of now photos, the old woman with her cat, Catholic. The meaner

I got the more he wrote. He is in the car financing business. 10 years in Germany after the war. His office is decorated with photos of me. His staff calls me ancient. So, like a vain fool, I wrote that you 1933 were much more attractive (he was born in 1918), and Don the Marine 1930, and Bill at 17.

But then in his last letter, last Saturday, John wrote, "Yesterday while travelling by tube, sitting opposite me was a girl who could have been you at 24...I had to speak to her, and I shall meet her again. When I kiss her it will be like kissing L. B. Probably better, because Americans are notoriously bad kissers (etc)....."

You see what this did to me. Even in letters I transmit something I call dead. All my priests warn me and laugh at me.

So I wrote today this "caracter" to take up life and leave me alone. Me for Suzy, gin and scribbling. Jan and the world for doing.

Lotti is coming to Rochester and I have asked her to stay with me. I can sleep on the couch in the sitting room. New curtains for the bedroom and dust ruffle of blue and rose on cream. For her beloved coffee, a little Japanese bamboo cup, an English bone Tulip cup, a Dutch blue and white egg cup. All the things I would do for you except that Rochester won't have it. Be a good boy and keep your neck straight and your back long.

This de Lungo did do me a great favor. Telling him that my next essay would be about Mary Pickford and gentlemen screwing little girls (my first love affair at nine), John mentioned LOLITA. I got the book from the library. All true. And also what nobody has believed about Carroll, Ruskin, Dickens, when I said it. The reason I can hang the tale on Mary Pickford is that she was *not* one of us...she sounded the warning.

Ever since my new teeth, caps, and costly replacements, I have grown thinner. What dread disease? But I suppose it is just not eating. Suzy sends you her love, but Henri said that she was the most wonderful cat in the world... and she has brown hair —

Brookstein

In June and July letters from Louise, lengthy and meandering, rained from the sky. Most were sent Air Mail. The postage was 7 cents from Rochester to Toledo. A letter got there next day. Moreover, if one going from Toledo to Toledo was posted in the morning, it was delivered that same afternoon. Our carrier walked the same route twice a day. Such was the postal service then.

I took a break from literary labors for a trip to the Big Apple. Lee Anna Deadrick at Macmillan offered a contract for a children's book. I had found the perfect artist—a lady who never knew a happy Halloween as a child.

Therefore she made a habit of dressing up as Witch or Clown to paint delicate eggshell tempera self portraits. When I visited, I got the suit she didn't wear. We were to meet at Macmillan.

Miss Deadrick glowingly praised sample pictures the lady (dressed in modest everyday garb) brought— exquisite drawings in silverpoint. Then announced they were on the wrong sort of board and must be redrawn. The artist, who'd also traveled from Ohio, rose from her chair. She snatched back the pictures, put on her coat, declaring in an odd tone, "I'm an artist, not an illustrator. Jan, I'll meet you across the street." And walked out.

Without the artist, Macmillan withdrew their offer. Downcast, I met the artist at Longchamps Restaurant, and she asked if I wished to run away with her. An odd proposal.

Retreat to Toledo. No contract.

Dear Professor Wahl   Friday 16 June 1961

Eight suffering hours it took me to copy the script. It is the only fair copy I have don't lose it or I shall arrive by broom stick to pound you on the head.

Remember, you will be my only critic—oh, I forgot, when Henri was here Jim DID read pages 15-21—out loud. I wanted Henri to know for sure that Jim's "pregnant silences" did not tell the truth, in fact, nothing. But there goes my Sennett gag.

I don't want any wonderfuls or lousys—Lotti and others do that. I want page and line for spelling, structure, fact and truth.

If it is dull anywhere — tell me. I tried to cut it to 20 pages but it is forged from beginning to end with invisible links. The three TRIUMPHS. OUTSIDE LOOKING IN and BEGGARS OF LIFE. Wellman and my refusing to do PUBLIC ENEMY. Peggy Fears. And why Menjou did Lubitsch, not CHAPLIN.

**************** **** ******** ** *********

You are the dearest, most thoughtful and generous boy and I am an abominable old bitch to blast you. I am sending you a little present from my Curiosity Shop. For future blastings.

The Pickford and Belasco's are marvelous. Now that I have no Eastman House for books, stills and films that damned Card can you suggest any books for research?

You mean you paid money for those squeazy Craig things? No, Beerbohm never quite came up to his opinion of himself. Nabakov was your teacher... Humnm! He knows his racket but that old intellectual dodge of pretending that filth isn't filt. Shit is shit in a backhouse or in a Sevre chamber pot.

Isadora Duncan, by Gordon Craig, Leipzig, 1905. Jan Wahl collection.

And don't give me any of it in your criticism.

I'll scream anyway so you may as well tell the truth—PUT THE QUESTION and I always cool out and do better.

> Love
>
> Lou

(handwritten P.S.:)

And return it Soon — Anxious

Obviously, she was in a clear-headed mood, and was waiting for a response to her essay from Lotte Eisner.

I sent her some lovely photo portraits of a very young Mary Pickford (pre-Griffith) cuddling a kitty, another with a white rabbit, publicity pictures when she appeared in stage plays for David Belasco.

I mentioned I acquired from A. J. Pischl of the Dance Mart the set of six studies of Isadora Duncan (in all save one, dancing) done by her lover, the radical British set designer, Gordon Craig, when they lived in Leipzig in 1905. They had no furniture, so slept on rose petals strewn on the floor.

I had loaned Jim Card the first edition of *Lolita*, Olympia Press, bought for me in Paris by my Danish chum Poul Malmkjaer. At once Louise linked together the author with his character Humbert Humbert, adding Ove Brusendorff whose expertise was more sex than film.

On Saturday June 17, *the mood soured. This letter, addressed to* "Junior," *begins:*

LOLITA has made me madder than anything since Ove's ART book. (Incidentally, Henri told me that Ove sent the book to a 14 year old neice of Henri's.) This Nabokov looks like Ove. He must have Ove' s book. It would make perfect illustrations for LOLITA. But to think this silly shit

TEACHES. Does he masturbate in class and get "The hollow of my hand still ivory—full of Lolita —?
Because he is gifted and wildly funny.

Vladimir Nabokov was a teacher like no other. His regal, white-haired wife Vera sat admiringly in the front row. When she laughed, we laughed. Nabokov stood on a kind of platform. We were studying *Anna Karenina*, which he told us was correctly titled *Anna Karenin*. Naby loathed the Constance Garnett translation and once spent the whole hour reading aloud to us in the Russian language to show how Tolstoy's rich music was lost.

When, one morning, he spoke about the closing scene at the train depot, when distraught Anna throws herself off the platform, he scurried down, grabbed his wife Vera's big purse, slipped it over his arm and became Anna—pacing, pacing, watching the monster coal-burning engine pull away. Watching, waiting, waiting, then leaping onto the tracks to be crushed by the wheels. *Threw himself down,* landing in our midst. We never forgot the end of *Anna Karenina.*

My adviser asked why I wanted to sign up for the Nabokov course. "He doesn't even have a Master's degree," he sniffed.

"He's our best writer," I said.

Louise continued her diatribe.

So IF you think you are going to shock me or anyone over 9 with your book you are not only wrong but stale as the men's toilet at Glennon's.

She concludes:

I have grown so accustomed to writing that I must get at something and stop writing these silly letters.
                              The old Abominable Woman
                              Lou

2155 East Avenue
Rochester 10 NY
Wednesday 21 June 1961

Stinkpot

Before I start screaming.. Two things. No three. First, after 4 years begging to stop the running toilet, I looked in the tank, went to the hardware store, for 55¢ bought a bulb and put it in after several minor errors. Oh, wonderful to be self-sufficient. Two — Glennon called Sunday night, license suspended for ten days, off to Dublin and Paris. I said look in at Cinematheque Francaise, 3 minutes up. Goodby. Why did he call? Three, my Englishman writes pages saying that I must not cut him off, that he does not understand a thing, well half, what I write. And I say every truth with facts — which leads me to think, after your criticism that I can't write at all.

And NOW...I hope you remember your letter, for, I shall take it up as you write, as you wrote it.

And I said to myself as I slapped a stamp on my last letter to you, "If this doesn't make the little sonofabitch mad enough to tell me the truth then my name is not Mary Louise Brooks Sutherland Davis Therese Brooks."

It did. It is the first letter you ever wrote me that I wanted to answer. No icky wicky sticky Jan pot.

****

THE SOCIAL CELEBRITY still is interesting because it was done by Lee Garms, fighting Menjous. I was 18, Menjous, 40? To make him look young without bags, Menjoue had Garmes rib up a frame of blinding lights. We all had to wear a white make-up. Grotesque. So, you see how stupid you film historians are? German? Pure Menjou.

And the Clara Bow is terrible, but true. The picture of me was taken same day as the picture you used. Paramount, 1925. You see, in 1927, I was a quite wonderful creature. Sleek as a pussycat, I went to Hollywood. With books which meant

"Drunk, drunk, drunk, is the color of my true love's hair." Scream telegram, laughter.

(INTERRUPTION: ON THE FOLLOWING DAY SHE SENT THIS WIRE:)

WESTERN UNION
Telegram
Rochester NY   1961 June 22

JAN WAHL
2116 POTOMAC DRIVE TOLEDO OHIO
SCREAM SCREAM SCREAM SCREAM SCREAM

LOVE   LOUISE.

Friday, June 23 1961...At first I thought what good is Jan's criticism which is not about my piece but about what he thinks is in my mind arid his resentment of it. I said no single word against Gordon Craig who is simple home-made art nouveau talented honest — Maxfield Parrish how did he get into the act — a true visionary calm I do not like calmness. Just like my friend, Lester Sinclair. Calm ... and do you know anymore about Les and why he is calm, homemade art nouveau?

I am not writing biographies, these are clarifying examples...Colman is my favorite actor. Why is his only alternative dear Noel?

Have read my whole life before you were born. Duncan was a great personality. Why must you insist that she was a great dancer. There is not even a foot of film for an opinion. She was first on the freedom train tooting the whistle. In 1890 there was no standard of dance. Everyone who wanted to be some one became a dancer. Today it is singing. 50 years from now some Jan will be saying that Elvis Presley was superb and some old Brookstein that he stunk. Nowhere *in piece did I say Izzy wasn't great.*

You know too much about writing to believe what you read. Genius is creative. Izzy a drunken little cunt who shook down everybody and gave all to a Russian who gave her syph in return was the peg to hang visions on. Name dropping is a naive and not very bright thing for a kid who has been around like you.

Those dancers who agree with her theories. What are her theories? Name one of Martha's theories. She would be the first to want to know. Despair is her motivation. What despair? What motive? You kids write for each others amazement. Krapauer. And who the Hell are Arnheim and Pudovkin?

To go back an instant, Jealous of Izzy? I who worship excellence above all else? And physically? A face like a melted dish of strawberry ice cream and a fat blubbery body with those long swinging tits? As for her art. She was as dead as a doornail by 1920. These are personal criticisms. Yet she is in my article without a single ugly word and I can think of a thousand wonderful things to say about her. But I am *Not writing Biographies.*

Ruth St. Denis I detest. She grabbed everything, lighting and drapery movement, musical "visualization" from Loie Fuller. and Izzy not forgetting the use of great music. *Yet nowhere do I knock Ruthie*

Nowhere do I say that I like Martha's dancing better than *ballet.* I am a Pavlova kid myself. My last dances 1941 were as delicate as Debussy. It was Martha who shook up ballet gave it fresh material and brought it commercial success again. "Stifling"? Some law that everyone must dance like Martha? If anyone spoke as foolishly about books — that they could only like what you like — Die for Earth Mother? I'll Die for Nabokov.

****

If, with the final paragraph in mind, after 10 months and 5,500 words I could not make it plain to you, elongating that bit, adding a paragraph or two or a 100 pages would not help. (THE BOX OF PAND0RA is what Mr Pabst and everyone on the picture called it.)

But I will try...

Chaplin showed me that movement is the foundation of acting.

Pride (at the bottom of all mistakes) made me try to get rid of it *completely.* The wiggly walk.

Then with Bergson, little children, Chaplin, Colman, Barrymore etc I show that mechinized movement ruins the actor. And I punch it up by showing that *pride* is also the root of one walk that we won't get rid of—O'Brien and Gaynor.

Pride is at the root of bad direction. To make cry. To make faces. Wellman and Mal St Clair.

A right walk made it possible for Pabst to cut a long scene to a few feet. Emotion he could get out of anybody. No hug.

And I when it came to the point instinctively *put away pride* and *walked like Lulu.* Application of the Chaplin lesson——Chaplin who *only* made wrong movements in the *world* of *Pride.*

Oh, this is a waste of time, and I must go to the store to buy Suzy some pussycat food and...

But don't think I don't love you for your criticism. It showed me that No person is detached from any kind of writing. The Essay is Brooks. And you made me think through the whole article which I had written to lead the reader's mind to his own conclusion and you are proof that I did good. You little muggywug

Love
Mudmother Lou

Lee Garmes = one of the top cameramen. In 1926 lensed Louise in THE SHOW-OFF. Memorable films—SHANGHAI EXPRESS, SCARFACE, ZOO IN BUDAPEST. He was equally outstanding using Technicolor, THE JUNGLE BOOK with Sabu a prime example.

Menjous = Adolphe Menjou. She gives various spellings. Vain by his own admission, his 1948 autobiography is titled *It Took Nine Tailors*.

O'Brien and Gaynor = George O'Brien and Janet Gaynor, the stars of Murnau's *Sunrise*.

Louise grudgingly adds:

Gordon Craig — I do not write about people I do not admire. His failure in all the arts gave him great insight.

And,

Lolita — now that I have gained my point. Jerkoff is marvelous. And what a story-teller.

2155 East Avenue
Rochester 10 NY
Monday June 26 1961

Dear Jan

The fresh notebook I took for the Lolita quotes is numbered Q. If I had not done some Lewis Carroll research for Pickford for Word & Movement which I decided not to use but save for the GIRL CHILD IN FILMS and written of it to an unknown Englishman who answered, "Oh, you must mean the LOLITA complex" I never would have been sent by the Holy Ghost to direct my mind these last ten years trying to learn to write. It's a natural — Ruskin-Proust-Nabokov.

And like Proust I read LO front, then back. Reading backwards is the best way. Of course there are hundreds of words I don't understand and thousands of connections and allusions but it has filled me with inspiration and confirmation and set me on the track. That Goddamned Card. That is his last Card. That finally discovering that I was not only on the level with writing but able to get a piece published he would cut me off from Pratt**Eastman House**thus driving me back to New York where I can get books and stills and see 100's of films on TV and around at all the film societies.

Humbert Humbert Germanizing Card who also takes his plots and characters out of movies. But he, not being a genius and I, not a character in a novel or film have not been as destroyable as he fondly believed.

The whole key to Naby is on page 267... The whole problem of fictional characters brought to life, changing like the living is set out. How he has succeeded with Lolita 12 to 17 is something I haven't worked out. But in real life I am succeeding but not with my old established audience. "Poor dear Brooksie" at the very moment lovely friends were waiting to fish me out of the East River. At 54 to Escape! Most ungratifying. Surviving Mr Flower at 9, Mr Vincent at 14, and George Marshall whom Mr Pabst believed had given me the final snowballing — well she was still young and beautiful and good for a whore for a while. But to take up writing — the beautiful and dumb — serious stuff — of course Jim writes for her, "Now, don't kid us, Jim, WE know." To refuse to write a hypo Confession which "the editor can put in shape for you."

And you too being woven into the Naby mystery. He is our good Angel. By 1966 you will be Jan Fitzgerald Wahl and I will be Gertrude Brookstein.

And I wrote Lolita in 1951, NAKED ON MY GOAT. To get my life from 7 to 17 off my chest (people even the foulest degenerates recoiled in horror when I talked about it), to learn something about writing. And then heave down the incinerator chute.

And now Naby has gotten Card off my chest (oh my). Without knowing Card I could not have completely understood HH I could not have cleared up that blind spot that allowed me to fall into Cards trap again and again. Everything he did was as predictable as a Western but I was hung up on the question Why should anybody want to destroy anybody who means them no harm. WHY should he want to destroy me? And then HH showed that there is an art of Distruction just as there is an art of Creation. The latter recreates what is beautiful in him in a work of art. The former destroys the person he hates, himself, in the destruction of another person. Which accounts for what amazes me about Jim, that he is without any remorse except a blubbering self-pity which he enjoys just like I enjoy a hangover. That is when he is out of action, in pursuit of no prey. HH retired to a nuthouse. Jim retires home with nurse wife. In action, like the creative artist, the destructive artist knows no good or evil, no fear in pursuit of his object. Bless Naby.

Of course the last half of LO is the book building to those two magnificent scenes. First finding Lolita and feeling satisfied that he was above God in being able to destroy her soul. The one thing he feared that she might yet go on to become a tennis champion he covers with the glasses — too blind to play. No, she is with No... "pointing with an invisible tennis racket."

I think the forward is a mistake. Killing her off for sure and allowing him to escape execution — No, I am wrong here — too full of the book still.) I keep forgetting it isn't true like Joan Crawford who built 30 years fame of experiences with everyone from her stepfather to the most bestial curs of Hollywood. And the movies LO wouldn't make.

And that murder of Clare Quilty. Tell the truth that's how it is with one ginloaded pervert killing another morphine loaded pervert. I knew Que too. Was John Colton — *Rain*. He was drinking ether at the time. "Make every bullet count." That spurt in the air from the piano stool. That's how death is. No relaxed plump with a hand to the heart but hideous, grotesque, absolutely unreal. Did you see the news reel shots of the Cuban executions?

Yes, as Naby says, "the esthetic bliss of art."

I have about 300 pages to write about his dialogue, Charlotte, and those gorgeous gorgeous words. He hams it up in the end piece. "No moral in two." Forward yes. He is a tricky one but he always gives you the truth and then teases you with a lie. I know after 15 years he found it unbearable to exhume LOLITA to put the Published story on HH. But it would have been marvelously funny and he is a poor straight writer compared to his novel.

I cannot believe that 4 publishers rejected the novel. And dared to tell him how to fix it. And he had to go to Paris. We all wind up in Paris.

I can't wait to see the Picture. They will murder it.
When is it to be released? I ought to subscribe to Variety.

Love

Lou

Finally God blessed Nabokov in Louise's eyes. ("He is our good angel.")

The entire letter is devoted to her revised opinion of the book, possibly the most important novel in English in mid-Century.

HH = the main character, Humbert Humbert, who is fixated on the underage beauty. Vladimir Nabokov revealed he could have had an American publisher before Putnam's took it provided he made Lolita an adolescent boy. So they wanted another *Death in Venice*?

2155 East Avenue
Rochester 10 NY
Tuesday June 27 1961

Dear Jan

I just checked your AFTERNOON OFF. Jan, you have everything to be a great writer or I would not be your friend. People without art do not interest me. But Jan, I told you before — you are not a girl you can't write out of a girl's mind. The moment you put your self on that spot the reader, if she is a girl or woman begins to ask questions and the answer is always NO. A man finds it just dull. Daydreaming in words. Having yourself. If a piece does not arouse sharp reactions it is no good and to hell with exquisite imagery. Like the letters you used to write me — dear sweet little Jan pot with a couple of fascinating touches of violence and sex.

That is the wonder of LOLITA. Naby never makes the mistake of knowing one Goddamned thing about Lo. He is Naby. He is Proust. Observing, testing, analizing, guessing, and *ALWAYS* being out-foxed. I used to laugh my head off at Card. He thinks he is brilliant. The easiest kind. Remember how I tricked him into not going to Paris? Not going to New York and yet at the same time sending down BEAUTÉ?

You must write about yourself. You will know when it gives you intense pain to put it on paper. And then all of a sudden you will be free and happy and wonder how you ever could have written like all the other kids in the same flow and subject matter.

Of course it is PRIDE PRIDE PRIDE that raised my ire. Pride is what motivates my every act.

And I have an idea from *your* ire about Izzy that those SANDS are pretty shifty.

And I am not writing a handbook to ballet or the art of Izzy or anything for you "to comprehend by your nature." You go on criticizing something you cannot even look at. Like the Movies and dancing and everything else you are expert in. No wonder pictures stink today. They are governed by a bunch of idiots who want to get in on the act.

"They won't (my insight, you can use it) even know how Lillian Gish acted with her *hair* nobody had such expressive, worried, demure, frightened, etc. hair as she did." Does that bring any pictures to your mind? I can't see frightened hair except as a fright wig. Do you think future generations are going to get a picture of Lill's "demure" hair from such stuff. Words words words fancy words to take in yourself and the other fancy worders. Do you know why you all write about things you know nothing about? When you know nothing about a thing, not knowing whether you are right or wrong, any general meaningless word that's different will do... When you write about something you know every fact every word snarls at you till you get it right.

Taking that silly story from Jim about Mr Pabst directing the fete scenes in BEAUTÉ. Anyone from the producer to the grip boy knows that even when they take a director *off* a picture they spend a fortune letting him crank on an empty camera until they can get a replacement.

Back to hair. Did you ever see Martha Graham in the middle of a dance swing her long hair to the top of her head in a knot? Do you know how many different ways Garbo does her hair in Camille? In what scene — only one — she dresses it just as in the opening?

I am going to do a piece on Camille. Of its kind it is the most perfect picture in the world. On the wings of her inspiration Garbo lifted everyone to genius. It is the Death of the Swan. She even falls to earth in a white heap in the country scene. And her death scene. The only time on the screen when an actress actually changes before your eyes. And dialogue no longer bothers her. She throws it away. And that end whisper......

Did you ever have long sticky hair in a wind and at a temperature of 110?

SIGHT AND SOUND.... G&G.... page 15.... about THE WIND

"Her hair was either piled up in a dateless fashion on top of her head or swirling round her throat and shoulders, more tormenting than the wind."

Oh, you are marvelous for me. Keep at me. I must learn to be good. Say anything that comes into your head. It makes me think think think.

You see, Lotti kept after me and after me to write and I thought I stunk and could never learn and she said, "Write it article by article and then you will have your book the way I did."

Present for Jan

Tomorrow I am going to my curiosity shop to my darling little Irene. She is a twisted hunchback and I make her laugh and act and dance and she is adorable anyhow. Forty years ago Mr Culver who owns the store found her a little waif about to be fired as a waitress and adopted her. In the Thousand Islands. "Florence, where can you be?" My favorite song. If I ever make any money we will go there and find out what the dressing is like.

Love

Lou

This letter, too, Jan, gives me great pain. But I want you to be great. And I want you to tell me the truth about the Dreyer piece. I haven't seen it the picture so I am a sucker. Did you write it before you saw the film?

Oh, it makes me ill to think so. But sometimes Jim tells the truth and he did see the picture. Tell me. Because now I beleive Jim. So it can't be worse. Who are you writing for? And I have a guilty consience because I mentioned ONE picture in my article I haven't seen. Oh Jan, Art is truth. Until every word is wrung out of you like LOLITA you are just playing games with the rest of the fakers.

(*handwritten:*)

Send me Lindsay's book

I'll return it -

Two single-spaced (separate envelopes) letters typed in one day! Must have taken hours.

Louise was pondering my "A Nun's Afternoon Off." A bit gentler on me now. But I disagree: in writing and acting you become something you are not. It's called empathy.

Willa Cather wrote one of the strongest WWI novels, *One of Ours,* through the filter of a soldier fighting in France in the trenches. The poet Walter de la Mare wrote *Memoirs of a Midget* and was neither a woman nor a midget, nor did he live in the century in which his heroine lived.

Yes, I objected to Louise calling Isadora Duncan a lousy dancer. For one, Louise only saw her at the end of her career, when "Izzy" was overweight, past her prime. L. B. described her as shaking like a bowl of jello.

Don't know which of us, Louise or myself, suggested first that Lillian Gish (Garbo too) acted with her hair, used in the Gish & Garbo piece. Miss Gish did it as early as 1913 in Griffith's *The Mothering Heart* when, as the mother, she leans down over her dead baby's crib. We don't see her face, just the hair hanging down. In every scene in *Camille,* Sydney Guilaroff at MGM gave Garbo a different hairstyle to support each mood. And Guilaroff was the one who convinced Louise to make Chinese bangs her trademark.

Maybe Jim *was* correct: the "fair" scene in *Prix de Beauté* has an intensity not felt elsewhere in its eight reels. Pabst may have visited and influenced this scene. However Louise was there and ought to know.

Poet Vachel Lindsay wrote an influential book, *The Art of the Moving Picture,* published by Macmillan in 1922, in which he saw that *Caligari* turned movies, as an art form, around a new corner. Actress Lenore Ulrich gave me her copy.

Of course I saw *Ordet.*

In Denmark before I met Louise.

2155 East Avenue
Rochester 10 NY
June 27 1961

Jan darling I don't want to hurt you I want to make you think...I wrote a short story about me in the Scandals chorus when a famous columnest wrote me up without knowing my name and another chorus girl said it was she and I called him and he said me and did I fix that girl but good. Because all the girls hated me and said of course it was she. WHO IS THE EXOTIC BLACK ORCHID. (from *Naked.*)

Jim read it and said it stunk but he couldn't say why and I didn't know how to fix it. So I quit trying to write fiction because I didn't know what I was doing. And I felt terrible. But I didn't get sore because success is a succession of failures.

And how I wept when Herbert Brenon called me a lousy actress on the set before everyone. And Martha

A Social Celebrity (1926). Scott Schutte collection.

used to make fun of my figure and Charlie Weidman and Mr Shawn would do funny imitations of my dancing.

And when I tried to make Jim do what he was capable of he would give me a black eye. That was before Naby made me understand that Jim was dedicated to another art.

If I can force myself to read it...I did...I am sending it to you right now. *Black Orchid*

You darling you have stirred me into action. Keep insulting me. But PLEASE read what I write....

Your letter "As for the three panelled mirror-looking." I didn't say anything about 3 p.m. I didn't shrug off *Afternoon Off.* I didn't think I had the right to criticize and I wouldn't lie when it comes to your most precious gift. And you are "tough" or I wouldn't scream at you. I read a piece Pratt wrote Real Trains Real something something. It was a mess of research put together a la very pansy Max Beerbohm. I went through it word by word and showed him how by doing some research on Porter and cutting out the show off stuff to prove how well-read he was and that silly index at the end you know 1, 2, 3, he could work up a conflict and make a point. But no he sent it off to the boy in California for the magazine and it came back and he Pratt blamed me. And he is right but for the wrong reason. He can't write. And I inspired him to do the article.

Yes, that was mean of me to pan Craig's drawings. I keep things about me for the same reason. Call me Downsy. And I loved your Elmer Forcefulfinger. You see at heart you are a mean funny sonofabitch and be it. Do you want to wind up a dull phoney like "Germanizing" Jim?

SOCIAL CELEBRITY.... "the kind of fact you ought to put in your book." In the name of Oliver Wendall Holmes that is the whole point of my piece to make "true revelations" whatever you mean by that. There is not a single thing in my article that you ever heard anywhere else. Are you sure you read it or were you too mad to see the words. I over did it.

"How the body expresses –" All that crappy Crapauer double talk. The people you can impress with that junk aren't worth it.

"Martha is an abstraction." What in Christ's name does that mean? My article says as plain as your foot why we have no great dancers. We have killed off all geniuses or won't let them do there right job…Sammy Davis, Jr. And it is a great artist who finds other great artists and nurses them to success. Just as you inspire me to write.

The Nijinsky bit I can't make out. You're slap happy with Izzy. Get that book finished and get rid of her.

"I am a name-dropper?" I can't help it if the people I talk about are famous but I would not take anybody's word on anything. If I cannot judge it myself I don't talk about it. Lotti (who hates Mr Pabst because of the Nazi thing) had Mary rent a projection room to show me the 3 Penny Opera and Lotti said it was marvelous and I sat there screaming because Mr P cannot direct satire. Now offhand I had taken Lotti's judgement. And Lotti sat staring at me because I was panning my beloved Mr Pabst.

"I am a writer too, and this (?) is the way I expect to deal with the world." I hope not. Because that sentence makes no sense. Oh, dear little Jan, I KNOW YOU ARE A WRITER. And you should thank God for me. Living in that mess of phonies writing for each other and never facing up to anything. I want you to be published. Not some silliness that will haunt you. One day, Card actually said to me that he was ashamed of the trail of lies he had left behind him in IMAGE.

"You admit: you wrote the article for Lotte." I write everything for a specific person. And I am not satisfied till

I see every picture transmitted to another mind. Do you think I write like this to anybody else. I don't even answer letters. Why should I bore myself with Naby's, "Well I guess this and Well I guess that," perfect imitation. You write a story for Brookstein.

"Heavyhanded hint" nothing. A person who deceives himself is a fool. If I wrote a couple of poems and I have no more gift than a baboon and then wrote a book on poetry would you call me a fool?

Along too I am sending the priceless photo and note sent to me from Cherryvale when I was doing research on *Naked On My Goat.* Please send them back at once. I wouldn't trust them with anybody else. And as long as you are bragging about yourself let me say that you are Goddamned lucky to have the friendship of one of the most extraordinary women in the world and some day you will make a fortune out of my letters you little sneak. And I won't be here to even scream at you.

Could you have the note and photo copied so I can send them to Naby? I'll pay you back. If you know where Naby is or his publisher. Or you could send them to him and tell him about the incinerated 1951 NACKT AUF MEINEN BOCK. Bock literally translated means ram and Naby's town was Ramsdale.

(*handwritten:*)

And he would love that real name, Mr Flower — to say nothing of that note telling ME about him.

Love
Downsy

I have already mentioned WHO IS THE EXOTIC BLACK OR-CHID. Louise composed it in a style flavored with Anita Loos.

Crappy Crapauer = Siegfried Krakauer. His *From Caligari to Hitler*, Princeton University Press, 1948, is a seminal examination of German film in its heyday. He may have gone overboard hunting for hints of what was to come, in discussing the silent period. Germany fell deep into an abyss yet painters, poets, writers and sculptors all re-energized—particularly Expressionists.

And, like Paul Rotha's *The Film Till Now*, the stills were mouthwatering enough to get a teenager excited about the movies from this period. Krakauer gives a pretty substantial case for his theories.

Pabst made a stupendous satire with *The Three-Penny Opera*; Louise is definitely offbase. Everyone save for its curmudgeon writer Berthold Brecht praised it. Holds up wonderfully.

A neighbor lady on Main Street from Louise's hometown, Cherryvale, Kansas, in fact a woman whose family moved into the Brooks house after they left for Independence, replied in 1952 when Lou needed photo donations. The note stuck in my memory since it quotes Louise's mother as saying, "I would rather have cobwebs in my house, than in my brain."

2155 East Avenue
Rochester 10 NY
July 5 Wednesday 1961

Dear Jan

FIRST AND QUICK. You really must learn to read what I write in my letters. I DID NOT say that Jim said "you never *were* with Dreyer." He would never say such a foolish thing when your essay proved that you were. He said you wrote it BEFORE you saw the film. (For Image)

Even then I hesitated to tell you till I read your piece on me which contained various errors which you could have so easily corrected by asking me.

I know that it is pride and youth that make you say, "I don't give a hoot. I can only laugh." People's judgments are made up of other people's opinions. Until I actually started to write and *remember* I was panning Chaplin's life with the rest of the mob. And it was the nasty things Ove said about you that changed Jim's opinion of you. He has no opinions of his own. (And further, I still have a lingering suspicion about you.) Why do you think I went to such lengths to prove to Henri, Lotti, Fr Cousineau that Jim does not write my stuff? And George around for days? Wherever you think he has hurt you with people of use to you, look out.

And now a million thanks for copying my stuff. My English boy photographed the tenement where Chaplin lived in wonderful, clear, angled photos. Would you like to copy them? It is about to be demolished but people still live there and it is more terrible than anything in "A DOG'S LIFE."

The books came this morning. Those old bindings gave my heart a pang.

No, I am not going to do anything with NAKED. Naby made me think of it and gave me the courage to look back. As you know, ORCHID was only a rough draft of a chapter out of the book and that cut to the bone. Elsewhere I have Green screaming at the girls for body-painting themselves white, and brown like Mary. So her problem, if they had kept the Congo number in the show, was whether to black up and I probably would have put on a crazy make-up of some kind. No, I just wanted to see what you thought of it. And your conclusion agrees with mine. I didn't know my racket. It's such a marvelously fit title, one day I'll write it.

My list after I threw out that corny 13 title was ... C Bennett, Bow, Crawford ?, Davies, Garbo, Gish, Pickford, Shearer, Swanson, C Talmadge.

But after a hundred pages on Gish I found out that I am not the biography type. I get so sick of people on paper, just like in real life.

And then I read...V Woolf... "The best of a book (to a writer) is if it makes a space in which, quite naturally, you can say what you want to say."

So my book will probably bare the rare, imaginative title, Essays on Films.

Funny, I did a bit of work reading about Colleen Moore because Clara Bow learned her acting from Moore pictures and Moore was an excellent actress. But she is the damndest bore.

Somewhere, however, I must tell about the absolute fascination of her one brown one blue eye. I would sit and let her talk at me just to watch those eyes which gave me the feeling that I was talking to two different people with one voice. Dietrich I would love to write about but I met her only once when she first came over and was sweet and fluffy in baby blue. Same with Negri. Just once Mal st Clair took me to her dressing room and we were much interested in each other.

How nice to be compared with V Woolf, flatterer. What did you think of Hemingway, after killing everything else in sight, blowing his own head off. The right thing. I'm no fan of his though I think he was a fine stylist and certainly shaped the whole writing game of today. Bang, bang,

At first reading "My Fourth of July present to you," after all the mean things I've written you, I was expecting something that ticked and had to be immediately immersed in water.

My curiosity shop is closed till next Week. They are at their store in the Thousand Islands.

Love
Lou

Your wary criticism of the Black Orchid chapter with a mental lapse on the Pickford essay made me laugh very much. Had you read the Word and Movement with a hundredth of that attention and given me that? Perhaps on the other hand routine out of the hundreds of letters you must have received from publishers and editors I would have been pleased. My key figure, Queen Elizabeth, you did not even mention. As for NAKED...I burned that because my work was uncertain. But now I know perfectly how to write it. And no one in the world could tell me how. There would be no jobs for those suckers if people did not imagine they could write before they learned their trade, and after learning it have something to say. Two letters I have received, one from Macmillan, one from Random House, both of whom ASKED for my work and then wrote suggestive letters which prove that book publishing and publishers are even sillier and vainer and bigger showoffs and failures than picture people.

Look at Hemingway? He was finished in the 20's but he went on to make a fortune because, like Shaw, he had built himself into a million dollar prestige personality. This is essentially right because "It is souls that we are ever thinking about, it is souls that attract or repel us." But Hemingway remained a 12 year old boy playing with cap pistols and little girls as true and blue as LOU.

I have never known such happiness as writing because no other art brings me so precisely to truth and robs the personality of ego. Painting is wonderful in that it blacks out the world of the mind. But it doesn't solve anything. I put down my brush and all the questions are still there. Acting and dancing made me unhappy because they are all ego, competition, fear, envy.

In Search of Louise Brooks, to be published and reviewed in that middle-European Saturday Review, leaves me cold. As Gish said, "You have plenty of time." That is the great difference between you and me. You are young, you want fame, money, pestige and naturally so. But it ruins your judgment. You race along madly with the going thing trying to outviolence the violent, outsex the sexy. The thing that made me famous was Laotzu... "Cling to what is unique in your personality and never depart from it." And then I ran out of money. Returning to Hollywood they pulled out my eyebrows, downed up my mouth, dyed and curled my hair and as Goethe said they liked me even less. But my heart was never in movies. As my father said when I was still a small child "Louizie has to work alone, she can't work with people."

I have just been plowing through Strachey's QUEEN VICTORIA which for a reason I did not know I felt I must read for GIRL CHILD IN FILMS. There it was, from 18 till her marriage, Victoria was wildly in love with Lord Melbourne, 40 years older. The populace even cat-called "Mrs. Melbourne at her."

Maybe Lillian Gish will give me some leads in research. I wrote her how important BROKEN BLOSSOMS will be in the article.

I swallowed the Brooks vanity and talked to George Pratt about it. He is wonderful about books, but I doubt that he will help. Jim was on vacation but George talked as if the phone was bugged. He was quite nasty in good oldfashioned pansey. Implied that my piece which he had read in its early stages when I wanted to rehearse on some one was no good. Implied that the Cinematheque magazine would never appear. He still blames me for his rejected REAL TRAINS, REAL HORSES, *REAL EVERY-THING.* His is one mind that I can read through and through. If I had not got him excited in digging up stuff for me — he is also a mad Isadora fun — he never would have written the article, his first excursion outside IMAGE.

Do you have any material on Marguerite Clark? Or Navimova?

Love
Lou

Like Mr. Dickens, Louise can conjure up a lot in few words. A lesson to me.

This last letter, July 5, has much good stuff in it. Apparently I did an article or two in *Image.* I don't have them. They might have been full of youthful bravado.

In high school, for a composition, I wrote on *The Cabinet of Dr. Caligari.* The English teacher, Carrie Whaley, humiliated me by telling the class I must have copied from a book. Not fair. Some kids sang or danced, or were expert in sports—why couldn't I write?

I closed my eyes and thought, Mrs. Whaley, you mean old bat, I wish you were dead. Within a few hours her husband and she were killed in a car crash. That rattled me. The power of the word, spoken or silent.

Louise often rode a high horse to oblivion. Would she ever see a book, any book, to the finish? She had a habit of throwing her efforts away. *Thirteen Hollywood Women* was not to be.

It's true about Colleen Moore's eyes, one brown, one blue. They were mesmerizing! I met her in Chicago at her dollhouse display. Her orbs gave cameramen problems as did Norma Shearer's. It is claimed Norma squinted. Audiences never knew it.

I've deleted paragraphs on Proust and Goethe. As it is, probably you are skimming—to find the juicy nuggets.

George's piece concerned the Edison Films' pioneer Edwin B. Porter of *The Great Train Robbery* fame. A one-reeler that became so popular "Pop" Lubin from Philadelphia made his own version. Many claim Porter's is the first American story film. Not so, it was *Jack and the Beanstalk*, also by Porter. Made the year before, 1902.

Marguerite Clark was an enchanting, fey rival to Mary Pickford who starred in a magnificent art film by Maurice Tourneur, *Prunella*, in 1917.

Alla Nazimova = Russian-born actress who dared take on Oscar Wilde and Henrik Ibsen and in so doing lost her proverbial chemise.

One of fate's wee jokes: Nazimova was godmother to Nancy Reagan.

2155 East Avenue
Rochester 10 NY
July 17 1961

Jan

You are so right. But I don't care about being published. Painter at Macmillan would give me an advance in a moment. I want to take my time. That's all I have now. Writing. I don't want to beat some deadline. Lotti just wrote that the magazine will come out in the spring. And I don't doubt that the French government which could pay $4000 for my visit to France could get up another $100 for my article as she said.

Did you get my darling Chinaman on that smug bullock? I laugh to think of him.

Louise

I have just been typing up my Clara Bow notes, 100 pages. And since I know her so well and need no help, I think I will do her for a popular magazine while I am collecting stuff for Girl-Child....

Jan Wahl in Denmark. Photo by Ditte Halling.

Little Chinaman on a bullock, where are you?

He sat perched at each desk I had in Brooklyn Heights, in upper Sealand in Denmark, ultimately in Mexico—where he vanished—pixies broke into the place and stole my Mickey Mouse watch and among other coveted items, the Chinaman.

On a midnight moonlit night in Denmark, I'd just returned from chopping wood with Fru Halling (who years before saved me after Isak Dinesen fired me). The Hallings had a forest retreat, a cozy cabin constructed out of lumber from trees Edith, or Ditte, herself felled driving the bulldozer.

The Chinaman and I watched, astonished. Foxes stood outside the window in a precise line to poop simultaneously. It reminded me of gurus on India mountaintops who demonstrate even that can be beautiful.

Wait a minute!

Louise is a writer not giving a hoot if she's published? Emily Dickinson didn't mind having a home for a poem in a newspaper.

2155 East Avenue
Rochester 10 NY
July 19 1961

Dear Jan

Thanks for the photos. And look Jan, lets get one thing straight. DON'T DO ME ANY FAVORS. Last last favor, the article you wrote about me is the end. I don't like to be mean, but it is always the favors you do that get you into trouble with people. You be strictly on the level with me. Card, too, thought I would put up with any thing for the FAVORS he did me.

What a nag you are. Here are the slum pictures. Send them back and have a set of copies made for me.

Use the head you sent me March 30. The background steals the scene in the nice photo you sent today.

I have TOLD you. I have never sent de Lungo any photos. Will You Stop!

I could kill myself. Remember the record player sounded lousy? Well, this morning I decided I would get it fixed. The man came, pushed the needle back in position. $5......

Last night at two Bill Kendall phoned from New York. He was in love with me 30 years ago. Nobody, not even that bastard, George Marshall ever quite falls out of love with me. Bill had been to Glennon's so he called and talked for 40 minutes. He said he had a new house in East Hampton and John McClain (whom I have known for 30 years) lived next door.

Then this morning I was looking at The Saturday Review and saw Dorothy Parker's name (whom I have known for 30 years) and that made me think of McClain again because she once threatened to jump out of the window because he didn't CARE.

Why hadn't I thought of him before? He is a big lazy slob but he has always said I could be a great writer. So I mailed him my WORD AND MOVEMENT and said that I wanted an agent for THE BOW WHO TIED UP THE TWENTIES.

It's July and he is probably on vacation. He is the drama critic on the Journal American. But I took a chance. Because he knows what kind of man I could put up with. I have an agent now if I want — Nat Perlow — remember Mike Hall brought him to my show in New York. But his mind is set on the True Confession crap and I told McClain emphatically that I would not write such a book which, anyhow, if I listed all my famous love affairs, would be longer than WAR AND PEACE.

And try to be a good boy and don't annoy the old woman. I am furious. That bull has whatchamacallits and I didn't see them!

> Love
> B r o o k s t e i n

(*handwritten:*)

Where can I get those Chagall post cards —?

So that's who Nat Perlow was, an agent. Didn't look like the literary sort.

Whatever was popping into Louise's head flowed out through the fingertips.

Loulou's mood swings were roller-coastery. However she was urging me to stay with her. She worried over the impropriety of a young man's sharing the flat, though. Neighbors, landlady and Mother Digges might not approve.

She hatched a foolproof (she thought) plot out of an operetta from Vienna: I am to disguise myself as a girl. It knocked me for a loop. She was serious.

What would it have been like had I hung out with her? Instead, I decided to hang out with publishers. For the third time Harper was reading *Pleasant Fieldmouse.* Now where should I hang my hat temporarily?

Henri Langlois, Cinémathèque Française, Paris.

The Algonquin had been the spot for Dorothy Parker, Robert Benchley, Alexander Wolcott, James Thurber. Why not me?

I thought that might impress Harper's Ursula Nordstrom.

Here is my confirmation:

September 25, 1961
Dear Mr. Wahl:

Thank you for your recent note.

We are happy to reserve a single room and bath at around 13 a day, for your arrival Friday, October 6, departing October 10.

We look forward with pleasure to having you back with us here at the Algonquin.

Sidney J. Colby
General Manager

16 Buckingham Street
Rochester 7 New York
26 October 1961

Dear Jan

Your letter, postcard and squirrel (which I gave to the landlord's daughter) arrived all on last Friday.

This is a little street a few blocks from Eastman House, quiet, tree-arched, a 4 apartment grey board Regency house with white shutters and a blue door, a down stairs apartment, sitting room, bedroom and a large real kitchen with windows on the east. My cooking has improved. The terrible tension of that filthy house kept by Jukes with the hideous road construction, noise and dirt, has left me. Only a block to gin and beans. 20 minute walk to The Blessed Sacrament Church.

I wish there was something to say about your book. But as you say, who in Hell knows what publishers will publish? A good agent is the thing and yours sounds active.

Hayden Griffin of the Pat Sullivan Agency wrote me about representing me. Tell me what you know of that outfit — if any. They wrote Jimmie too, wanting him to do a book on me. He is interested.

Langlois sent me a beautiful catalogue with wonderful illustrations of the Melies Exposition at the Louvre. (His JOURNAL will be a beauty.) Langlois will be here, says Jim, the last of November.

Since I have been adopted by the Academy of the Sacred Heart and Mother Digges at near 55 my life is getting crazier and crazier. Sunday next, 9 o'clock mass in the chapel with the snobbish ladies who amuse Mother with their curious stares at me, breakfast, priests, lunch, chat-chat, benidiction and home at 4 PM.

About TIME magazine...now pay attention and do as I say.

In 1928-29, Lothar Wolff, then 19, did the publicity for LULU and DIARY OF A LOST GIRL. A Jew, he took it on the lam in 36? Then a cutter he made a picture in COPENHAGEN with Annabella and the Hungarian director, Paul Fejos who fell in love with A and presented her with a 100 pound box of chocolates. Woofie waited in Paris and then came on to New York where he became film editor for the MARCH OF TIME. Under Louis, then Richard de Beaumont. For the last 10 years and more he has been a producer — MARTIN LUTHER, PINKY — for Louis. He knows everyone on LIFE and TIME; and bark like a dog. . .Woof, woof, ask him.

Now, when you know your plans in New York, write Woof and say in a simple way with no baby talk that I told you to see him. Then follow the letter up with a telephone call for an appointment. You have my run-down and lots to talk about. He knows me intimately and you can say anything.

Lothar Wolff

Louis de Rochemont Associates Inc.

380 Madison Avenue

New York 17, NY

Oxford 7.0350

This address goes back to my last trip to New York 1960; Woofie is in the book.

Love   Lou

The constant daytime commotion across the Street on East Avenue, the construction that never seemed to stop, was too much, and she found a new place.

Meanwhile I was asking for no favors from her and accepted none.

I'd already approached de Rochemont's office, once, on behalf of Carl Theodor Dreyer. Maybe they might be interested in the JESUS-project. Dreyer said he was committed to Blevins Davis of Independence, MO.

I doubted "Woofie" had any clout with children's book publishers.

$13 a day! I couldn't stay at the Algonquin forever. Ursula Nordstrom at Harper promised a contract and my idol Maurice Sendak was to illustrate. But when?

My new agent was Candida Donadio and the first time I was in her office she stood there banging her head on the wall. It had taken her years to sell a novel called *Catch-22*. A literary critic, John Mason Brown, read a pre-publication copy and raved, "It's like Lewis Carroll writing *All Quiet on the Western Front!*"

So the publisher, who bought it mostly because they needed a war book on the list, had called to say on pub day they'd have sky-writing planes over the skies of L.A., Chicago and New York spelling out the title. Hence the head-banging. Publishers were ditsy and so were literary agents.

With a children's book I was small potatoes. "They'll give you more than it's worth," Candida snapped.

The only person I knew from Toledo was Gregory Markopoulos, the experimental filmmaker, a long-time friend. He lived in the West Village on 11th Street. Like Maya Deren and other leaders of the American avant-garde, he worked in 16mm, preferring Kodachrome. He had dark Greek painterly eyes, and composed ravishing shots in films that were to include *Flowers of Asphalt, Twice a Man, The Illiac Passion* and *Bliss*.

He had just returned from Greece where he filmed his first 35mm feature, in color, *Serenity*, on a budget of $50,000, a fund collected from his father's shop-keeper friends in the old Greek section of Toledo.

The film was shot silently, then Gregory had three professors from Columbia, one speaking English, one Greek and one Chinese, narrating the track. No, Louise. I never saw the completed film. Gregory cut it apart and tossed out any continuity.

Then spliced the thing together based on images, not the soundtrack. It was sensational to some. To the backers a puzzle and a headache.

I had barely got in the door of his pint-size apartment when Gregory demanded, "*Lend me $10!*" Seems he owed the first-class Guffanti lab, at 630 Ninth Avenue, a considerable sum for prints. He wanted to take a taxi and arrive in style. That way, in case they happened to look out the window, they'd think he might have money. Guffanti was many, many stories up.

To us common folk this wouldn't be a solution to not paying a bill but to Gregory it made perfect sense. I gave him the ten dollars.

And stepped into a loony bin.

Beggars of Life (1928). Scott Schutte collection.

16 Buckingham Street
Rochester 7 NY
18 December 1961

Merry Christmas, Jan

Where are you? I wanted to send you some of my New Improved Fudge made in a sunny kitchen with a view of pink curtains in bed and sitting room. Or are you in a sulking cycle? I hope youre in New York getting your work published.

John McClain, "slow but not neglectful," sent my WORD AND MOVEMENT to his agent, Kenneth Littauer, of Littauer and Wilkinson, who wants to handle me and asks where to offer the piece. But neither Lotte nor Henri will say I can publish it here. And if I did try to sell it I could cut 5 pages with the Jap dancer and Ruskin, etc. Open fast with Garbo revolutionizing film movement.

I think I should get into my WOMEN with Pickford or Bow or Talmadge or Davies don't you?

Now stop playing idiot boy with the old Woman and write telling me whether you saw Woofie.

Card doesn't even call drunk anymore and George positively snarls on the phone – no, sneers – if I call for information, so I must give up all use of Eastman House and follow the advice I gave you.

John Springer sent me a piece he has done on me for that series. Very kind and okay. All my corrections were much more scandalous and crazy than his imagination. And I wouldn't dream of taking away the dramatic pity of that "little one room apartment" and wretched obscurity establishment by Card. YOU didn't have to anchor your piece on that.

Love Haste
Brooksie

Why does Louise picture me sulking?

The next months are somewhat of a blur; I bounced back to Toledo several times where I believe I spent Christmas. That's where she sent her letter. Anyway, holidays came and went and I slept on the floor at Gregory's abode.

For his *Twice a Man*, he used one woman, a striking-looking actress, Olympia Dukakis, who gave acting classes over in Montclair, New Jersey. Lithe, limber lads ran rhapsodically in the cramped quarters on 11th Street in bright red jockstraps. Many scenes were done in the apartment. The film was finished a year later.

There was an "extra" room—tiny with no windows. Rented out to a mystery man, Bob, who was gone in the day. By evening he sat rigidly upright in his room at a teeny tiny desk with a teeny tiny lamp in front of a teeny tiny folding bed. Bob was immaculate, everything just so. And never spoke. What he did at that desk I have no idea.

At night, on a thin shelf right below the ceiling, gleaming in the moonlight of the Spartan living room (which was painted in Grecian blue and white) was an impressive number of shiny black leather boxes. Gregory told me in a whisper they contained love letters from Jean Cocteau. His Eidelweiss.

One middle of the night the weight from the shelf was too much. All came tumbling, crashing to the bare floor. A naked Gregory rushed in, weeping, *"My Edelweiss! My Edelweiss!"*

The letters and, some photos flew in all directions like winged paper birds.

I pictured my letters to Louise fluttering through the room on Rockingham. I wondered what she might call them.

16 Buckingham Street
Rochester 7 NY
26 December 1961

Dear Undeserving Epiphany Boy
    Your fudge is in the works. The only box I have is the one June sent with the fruit cake. But I will try to lump your 12 day's worth into it. All those little brothers! Mine could smell fudge a block away and find it hidden in the attic eaves.
    Your "Spanish Christmas" sent me to the Catholic Dictionary where I read that after the 4th century the Eastern celebration of the birth of our Lord was changed to Dec. 25. Unless you are a dissident Armenian——living in Toledo—— that would explain a lot.
    Thanks for the KREPLAH. Is it one of your children's stories?
    And the Isadora Duncan phamplet. It is full of good and useful stuff. ~~XXXXXXXX XX~~
    ~~XXXXXXXXXXXX~~ (I must have my mind on shelling walnuts.) The more an adorer extracts and rounds out, the more she reveals. As a con artist Izzy had no equal from her earliest years. And when she hit on the idea of giving the "Intellectuals" who could no more write about dance than I can about music — their old stuff back to write about — painting and Botticelli, Goethe and poetry, Beethoven and music — she was IT. So you see you are not really defending Izzy and her dance which you could not judge without seeing — you are defending your ancestors.
    Like Cardinal Newman (I am reading his Apologia Pro Vita Sua) who tried to reconcile the 39 Articles with Catholic doctrine and talk the English into going back to discipline and doctrine after Power, Greed and Prestige had bloodied England for 400 years reducing the church to

a National Institution. And they call Catholics dreamers. After Newman became one the way he was dodged about, hidden away, occupied with nothings till he was too old to fear and they graced his brilliance and goodness with the red hat. "Lead kindly light."

But you, my little writer, why don't you do what every creative worker has done since forever — turn your canvas to the wall and turn your mind to a new work. In the meantime, if something good happens to DANCING ON THE SHORE, wonderful. But I have seen that everywhere XXXX a pushy artists works against himself. For neither the pushed nor the pusher is really sure and they get to hate the sound of each other.

My case is the opposite. I was so sure that Littauer (who handles only names) wouldn't want me, that I could just relax back, a comfortable failure supported by the Church and the gin bottle and now I must figure out what to do about WORD AND MOVEMENT and dig into the drivel and work up an outline of WOMEN IN FILMS. I'll get it off after the first of the year. It isn't the work I dread. But I read the reviews of all the acclaimed and the reviled junk in Sat. Review and why should I add to the distruction of forests?

What are your plans for NEW York? Write.

Love
Brooksie

(*In red crayon:*)

L. Gish sent me a darling Xmas note – and Glennon a great big pot of poinsettias, and my sister cake and St. John of the Cross, and my landlady – pleased with fudge – an almond coffee cake from a wonderful Jewish bakery – So you all made me feel very happy–

Jan Wahl in Greenwich Village. Photo by René Concepcion.

The KREPLACH story? It was an old Jewish joke about a boy who was afraid of Kreplach.

Louise told me Jewish jokes, so I wrote one to her. My favorite Louise joke is short:

"At a crowded matinee theater, a middle-age matron sitting with her daughter jumps to her feet shouting, "Is there a doctor in the house?" A handsome young man rushes up the aisle. 'You wanna meet a nice Jewish goil?'" Louise told it in her best Fanny Brice voice. Brooks *loved* Fanny Brice; said she was the smartest. I'm sure I'd love her, too.

Oh. She's still on a tirade about Isadora Duncan. Again, it's Loie Fuller and Isadora who turn dance around a corner and free it of tight ballet slippers and constraints.

When I returned to 11th Street, Louise's Twelfth Night fudge, sent there, was gone. Gregory shared with the boys in the red jockstraps. "We ate Louise Brooks's fudge," one of them boasted, making it sound like a sex thing.

Intelligencia of all kinds flitted through Markopoulos's world. Including Edgar and Louise Varèse. She was a well-known translator of French novels. He wrote experimental music. We listened, after a dinner of peanut butter sandwiches, at the Varèse flat, to an excruciating sonata composed for vacuum cleaners. He and she rolled their eyes in ecstasy as the French recording played. Edgar shouted, "René Clair stole from me!" (He meant a movie with Gérard Philipe.) "I never got a sous!" the composer grumbled. And put the record back on.

1962

16 Buckingham Street
Rochester 7 New York
4 January 1962

Dear Jan

I stubbed my damned toe staggering around in the dark and only my wonderful space shoes make walking possible. One of my teeth fell out and I have to go to the dentist too, this morning. So I will look in my curio shop and see about a letter opener. Years ago I had a beautiful Chinese brass one which Bill Kendall threw out the window of my room in the Madison Hotel in New York after I raised it in a state of irritation. And I didn't think to send for it in the court yard.

Reading Maude Adams for THE GARBO MYSTERY and GIRL CHILD IN FILMS, I came across this most perfect explanation of how the artist should regard his critic. She is writing Clyde Fitch whose play had laid an egg… "I feel so strongly that it is a turning-point for you and a hopeful one. I haven't seen the papers, but I know you…I have never seen anything funnier than some criticisms of a play I received yesterday, their abuse was funny (unintentionally), but there was no sting left—after one had read their praise—it was so absurd. But we can't afford to take criticisms of ourselves on the funny and absurd basis…Don't get in a groove. Make yourself agree with your critics for a time until you discover their secret—it is a secret to them as well—they can't put in words the real thing they criticize—they can't voice it—so you must discover it; but when you've discovered it you'll find there will no longer be need of it."

Love,
Louise

The ingenuous advice Maude Adams gave Clyde Fitch hits the spot. Well worth quoting.

Maude Adams is the most celebrated of Peter Pans—since the moment James Barrie conceived of a light-as-air boy who refuses to grow up. A pity Barrie's own favorite actress, enchanting Elisabeth Bergner, never had opportunity to perform the role in the German language.

It's a part that necessitates chutzpah. A custom has been that it's taken by a grown woman.

A number of famous actresses were bustin' out to play Hamlet; some actually did: Sarah Bernhardt, Asta Nielsen, Judith Anderson. Garbo could have done it. She wanted to be Dorian Gray for MGM.

In playacting, anything is possible. I've watched Jean Arthur and Mary Martin take Peter Pan on. Jean Arthur, middle-aged, had the lightness of touch. Mary Martin too earthy. Too Broadway.

For my money the best is Betty Bronson in Herbert Brenon's super Paramount production of 1925. I wonder if Louise would agree?

16 Buckingham Street
Rochester 7 New York
19 January 1962

Dear Jan

If I am a mean old woman, I am also a remorseful one, and although I know your wheedling tricks, by being a good boy you may (may, I say) get my Pogany.

I am so enraptured with THE LIFE AND LETTERS OF JANET ERSKINE STUART that although I am only half finished I had to peek at the end to see how she died. Like everything else she made an exhaustive study of dying and did it better than anybody.

Next to actress books nothing repells me like pious books and before Mother Digges knew me well she gave me one about a little Spanish nun who alternated folksy talks with Our Lord and His Blessed Mother with bang up beatings and rape by the devil. Except for a page here or their about her sewing—they had her cutting out uniforms on her death bed. The wonder to me is that any nun escapes being a Saint—four hundred sticky pages of such stuff were a great sacrifice to Mother Digges which I did not intend to repeat. So when she put JANET STUART into my reluctant paws I expected the worst. Not opening it I read first the sad, inevitable career of Maude Adams— at least pious books have happy endings—who did see to it that she got her reward on this earth. Now I understand the cool indifference of the Cenacle Nuns, when I spoke of Maude. She made retreats there, you know, and gave them her Long Island estate and saw it to that every penny was repaid in loving sweetness and service. If you knew what it is like to be served by them! I do. When I made the one day retreat at the Sacred Heart, the mothers, not the sisters, served our meals and I was torn between wanting to sink through the floor and wanting to stay on deck to watch the fat matron who, smelling me out as her natural enemy, had carefully deposited her creaking corsets at the end of the table, stuffed herself with the indifference of a pig at the trough. Happily, there was no talking and only two got a shot at me in the bathroom. But by noon I had cultivated a Mary Magdalen stare that turned away the boldest curiosity. Now I have no fears about my retreat there in July.

Loving nuns as you do, you must go to the library—the Sacred Heart Academy, maybe—and get Janet Stuart. The beauty of her writing defies description and her trip to America and what she had to say about us is hilarious. The sessions in Rome for the beatification of Mother Duschene with comments on the bishops in their private playpen!

But I must quote this bit I'm reading…"At Bologna I dragged the maiden all forlorn from the arms of her weeping parents, and when she had dried her tears she became like St Cuthbert's boy and 'never ceased expressing the thoughts of her mind' …which gave me occasion for many reflections.

"I heard that she was a novice tertiary of St. Dominic and …was obliged to explain that I, though unworthy, and not gifted with the star upon the brow, was at present Locum tenens to our Holy Father St. Dominic, until one of his sons could gather up the threads at Ostend, and say what should be done, so I have sustained her with hard boiled eggs and good advice and hope to tow her into port successfully in a few hours."

In this Order, the contrast between the Mothers who teach and the Sisters who do the house work is remarkable. The Mothers are the intellectual cream of nuns, the Sisters transparently simple. One day, sitting in the library with Mother Digges, I watched a Sister, done up in various dust clothes, come heaving in with much distress and helplessness to ask Mother what to do about the wax that dripped from the children's candles on the alter carpet. While she gave the Sister instructions my expression must have been less than charitable for Mother gave me a quick mortifying glance before returning to the book.

How glorious it is to be once more (after 6 years of stagnation among sterile minds and exalted pride) tried and tested, fired to effort by great intellects.

Oh, Jan, my sister, June gave $1050 to the Propagation of the Faith, 336 Fifth Avenue, New York 1, in my name from which I will receive 42 dollars a year for life and a set (10) of Gregorian Masses at my death. And I must say, the Suspense Card (Account No. *3791*) which I am to give to some one makes me feel rather out of things... "This is to inform you of the death of Miss Louise Brooks..."

But I wish you would keep an eye on me. You know, living alone and seldom seen, I could lie around rotting for days... And my sister has taken it upon her self to change my name, sending it about for various devotions to which she is addicted as Mary L. Brooks. I wrote her a sharp letter about this presumption, saying that I am Louise Brooks, dead or alive, and whatever religious effect she expected to put upon me with the name, Mary, should be forsworn. But she is not the brightest kid in the world and might class up, her mind, my tombstone. Keep an eye on her... All this for a lousy Pagany?

My brother is Ted Brooks, Wichita Eagle & Beacon, Wichita Kansas.

Love
Louise

The sincerity of Louise's faith shines brightly here. And Louise being Louise, she was quick to expose the hypocrisy of those hanging out at the retreat, not worthy of the Sacred Heart.

She almost makes me look up Janet Stuart, who had a sense of humor. It's a lack of it in religion that gives me pause. If God exists, given the cataclysmic perils strewn in our path to righteousness, He or She invented humor.

I hope the Willy Pogany found a happy home.

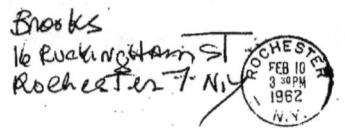

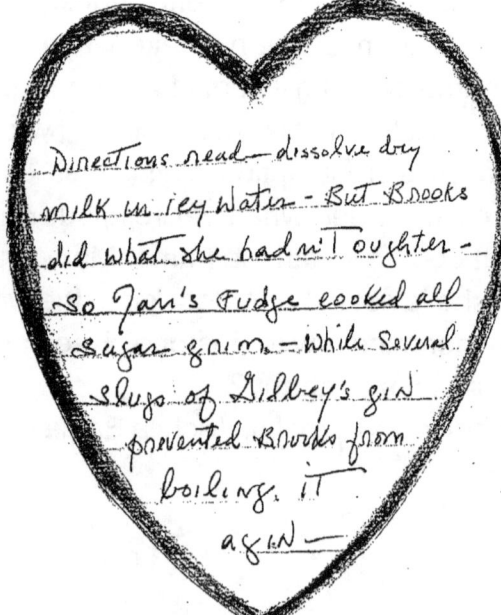

Winter in New York. Lots of snow.

Means no garbage pickup. Wienie skins and soiled napkins fly in my face. Indoors the city either is under-heated or over-heated.

If I can afford it, attending concert or play. Or going to poetry reading with Malanga. One time, Gary Snyder. Another, Ginsberg and his friend at the Quaker Meeting House at Gramercy Park.

No word yet on contract from Harper. Candida repeats: "They'll pay you more than it's worth." Are all agents that blasé?

I must escape from 11th Street soon; my funds are nearly gone. But I loved my home-made Valentine of February 10.

7 North Goodman Street
Rochester 7 New York
26 February 1962

Dear Jan

First, thanks for the Valentine. It was darling. And the SCREEN STORIES. John did a good job. And a sweet finish—if untrue. But quoting my letter almost got me thrown out of the Sacred Heart. Using Mother Digges name. I tore out that page and took it to her. Snorts and noises. Then a rereading and a wee smile at her name. This Friday she was quoting it—"God simply pulled me by the big toe…the yelps of healthy school girls." "But don't let it happen again."

Three days after I moved to Buckingham the crazy woman across the hall was giving me orders about the color of my curtains and the closing time for blinds. I told my landlord that she would drive me out, that I should move at once. No, no, he said, both she and her pregnant girl friend were moving. Five months passed during which they snooped and listened at my door—Suzy caught them—and I was quiet as could be, never letting a man in, never out after 5 PM. But when I first moved in and they were screaming about the thermostat conrol in my apartment—they knew I drank and they waited.

Monday, Feb 12, I drank some gin and went to bed at 6. At 10 the firemen were pounding on my door. They came in and threw some water on the smoldering foam rubber cushion in my chair and left. Without ringing my bell, knocking on my door, or calling the landlord to ascertain where the smell came from, the women had run screaming fire.

Then I stood in the door begging their pardon and asking them to forgive me for frightening them and endangering life and property. The husband of the pregnant spoiled wife upstairs snarled, "Leave, LEAVE, and RIGHT NOW." The two long grey hags across the hall stood screaming ecstaticly, "Drunkard, drunkard, drunkard." The lack of "whore" which all their snooping could never provide left their dialogue repetitious. And dead-eyed dick across from my door yelled, "You aren't fit to live with decent people. You ought to go off and KILL YOURSELF." (But don't mess up this joint.) The kind landlord arrived and they tore at him to throw me out right then and there. All night dead-eye patrolled my door in her joy and excitement waiting for me "to get drunk again and burn down the house."

Next day Landlord and I agreed that I should move. I meant it. He didn't, knowing the women would cool out and look forward to the next fun. As I told Mother Digges, if they could, they would have burned me at the stake. Before the "fire," they had complained because I had to shut the front door going to 6 O'clock mass.

I made landlord give me a rather sad list of apartments to look at. In less than an hour I was back with this charming apartment rented. He was confounded. I moved here on the 20th. Regular apartment building where I belong. 45 apartments filled with mostly lovely Jews intent upon their own business. Three blocks from the Treadway off East Avenue. And more wonderful. From my bedroom window I can see the lights go on at the Sacred Heart. And I am only two blocks from the Cenacle Chapel.

For eight years I have prayed to stop booze forever. Then Mother Digges took over and I got an answer. If the Buckinghams hadn't been on the look-out, I would have awakened at 11 and put out the smolder and gone on cheating. It was the cruelty of people without God, yet showing me myself breaking the commandment, "Thou shalt not kill," that did it. I bless them forever and left some expensive things I don't use—electric grill, fur lined boots, etc—for them. Their meanness about money and possessions is frightfull. My expense of moving again, useless new curtains, papering a wall there were part of their joy.

After Mother Digges got over her first silent rage with me she said what we both knew. "God has given you this great Grace. A new place and a new beginning which you can ruin with drink."

I wasn't sure till Sunday when I received Communion. Since I am not attached to people, bars and the licenses of booze, my big fight will be an occasion of fear— like Buckingham when I longed to crawl into bed with a bottle of gin and see oblivion. But however I am tempted I am finished forever. I knew it would be like this. Nothing repells me like A A, fighting that day by day crap. As if being out of your mind and scared half the time were pleasures to fight off.

I have taped three of my WOMEN IN FILMS for Louise Wilson's program here on radio. She is a good woman. We will do about 12 in all and she will run them in 6 minute segments over the weeks.

Also, Mother Digges idea for me to go to dinner with my confessor, Father Atwill (editor of the Catholic Courier-Journal). He and his two pals took me to dinner at the Dickens last Thursday. They are amateur actors and directors (not priests). Father shrunk to less than his 100 pounds while these kids gave out with every silly story that ever came from Hollywood. It was for me a sad evening—short—6 to 8:30—but the meaning will come clear.

Write and tell me what you are doing. I no longer need live like a jail bird and can see whom ever I please.

Love
Brooksie

Ever a Phoenix bird, Louise took the fiery removal from Buckingham in stride and adapted to her new cozy nest nicely.

I saved the March 1962 issue of *Screen Stories*. In the same issue Jane Fonda, Tony Curtis, Connie Stevens and Janet Leigh. John Springer did one of a series GREAT MOVIE STARS – WHERE ARE THEY NOW, in a nutshell telling her life. She "has won a reputation among serious students of the cinema as an actress comparable only to Garbo."

He described her as visible to passersby from the street into the midnight hours, tapping away on typewriter keys, putting her story on paper. He mentions two "notable" features, *Love 'Em and Leave 'Em* and *Beggars of Life*. Says she rebelled against the "system" and left to make films in Europe.

Springer tells how, in the Forties, he lived "across the hall" from a middle-aged woman with graying tresses and paid scant attention to her until once when, at Jim Glennon's bar, he noticed a page torn from *Vanity Fair* and only then connecting it to his un-neighborly neighbor now sitting at the end of the bar.

She was always alone, always aloof. And he met Jim Card, who lamented, "There is one great actress—if only I knew how to track her down."

After Card's "discovery" and invitation to Rochester, scholars according to Springer flocked to the door of a former little dancing girl presently smitten by movies she had once pooh-poohed.

They came from as far away as India, according to Springer.

31 March 1962
Rochester 7 New York
7 North Goodman Street

Dear Birthday Boy

Tomorrow will be my mass for you and a happy birthday year. Maybe it will be the year when you will grow up. I just grew up in February at the age of 55. It is wonderful. Being free of people. Not looking to them to flatter your sins. Not looking for ears to hear you and eyes to admire you. Not giving a damn for their opinions on anything. But the price is high. It's taken me ten years to get it up.

Janet Stewart wrote…."These things that come home to us and hurt our self-love and humble us in the dust—these are some of God's best graces. XXXXXXXXXXXXXXXX full, full of promise, and never think that you are at the end of them. There will come revelations ever more humbling, ever more intimate and ever more true. But never let them cast you down. Remember that they are birthdays, the putting away of the things of a child.

I am just finishing a book I have avoided for eight years. THE SEVEN STOREY MOUNTAIN. Not that I did not get some good pointers in religion—but time is growing short and that is a long, long book, getting longer and longer with his tiresome attempt to stick to a homely style and that boy's mind. He was only 33 when the book was published—10 years a Catholic. But it was fine getting a real look into that detestable school, Columbia. And he had two pals, Seymore and Lax—real jokers in the tradition of Charlie MacArthur and Company. The other thing that bores me besides his book reviews is his frightful overstatement. All places and things where I was at the same time very often—calling the dismal Streets of Paris in the Chicago Fair a very hell of vice. It is a book for boys and a very good one. But no more reading for other people's pride. – I know my books and my books know me.

If Louise Wilson hasn't given us another dry run—we had to re –tape three of my WOMEN IN FILMS—my stuff for her radio show ended. Poor creature, underneath her fear of being a hick and wasting her powers on acting like a real live celebrity she is a decent woman. When we began, my false front mislead her and she patronized me like crazy. But slowly whatever it is in me that frightens people wore her down to the point where she was slipping notes under my door instead of braving a phone call. And except when she called the Sacred Heart for my address which she had lost and I lost no time in telling her that the convent was not an answering service for actors—I have said not a unkind word to her.

But her radio dialogue is nothing but automatic responses to certain words or feelings. She did not study my notes or make any preparation for the interviews. When I wanted her to feed me a line or remind me of something she sat and stared at me as if I were telling her fortune. But just as soon as I had a particular point to make, she would start barking. Once, like a fool I warned her—a plug for my book. I said, "You know, actresses get pretty stale talking about themselves all the time, repeating the same thing over and over. They might take a leaf out of my book, WOMEN IN FILMS, and talk about OTHER actresses—but just one leaf because that's all I I've got written." And good old Wilson started barking on "but just one…."

However the taping has been great fun for me. I do imitations of Mr. Hearst's piping voice and Marion snoring through her own films. I do Bennett and Crawford and all screaming, "I certainly am NOT imitating Garbo's hair-do! Why, I'll have you know I've been wearing bangs since I was FOURTEEN!" I do the whole closet scene from Broken Blossoms and—in a word—talk just like me. Working out a theory about how radio interviews should live, not projecting a person afraid of the audience tied in knots— After 28 years, Wilson is so nervous that she doesn't even know what she is saying when she doesn't know what she is saying.

So much for marvelous me.

What are you doing in New York? Be sure to keep in touch with me. And don't go on peddling stuff old and outgrown. How can you even read it anymore? What was good as a kid? You should thank God that it is not published. If you are a true writer, that is. Or maybe you just want to be published and be somebody, anybody as long as you get the King for a Day pay-off.

Last end of February, I was Queen for a Day with Card because of the Screen Stories article. He also wanted to case my new joint. He arranged for me to see the Bow, THE WILD PARTY, her first talkie. He had Pratt and Steve on hand to play straight. They were mousy enough till I told them I was at BOOZE END. Then a subtle but fascinating change came over them. All the ugly experiences between us became purely the fault of my drunkenness— hand't I just confessed as much? It was wonderful to see them brighten and pass proud and complacent looks with Mother Card who by the time he brought me home was so at home with the new look that he said Father Cousineau "would be pleased" in a manner that left no doubt that he would give Father the idea that I was allowed to look at

Scott Schutte collection.

films with Father because I was a good old woman, a
reformed drunkard now. Father will punish. But aren't
people entrancing, especially when they think you don't
catch them?

My apartment is charming. Easy to keep clean.
After two months no one bothering me. And I love an
electric stove. My French bread is a toasty treat.

Love
Louise

Gregory asked to borrow $50; he explained he would spend half of
it at a fancy Greek florist on Madison Avenue, to wire flowers to his sister
Elaine who was a teacher in Toledo. The accompanying wire would
request a loan of $25.

I wondered if it weren't more sensible just to borrow $25 from me
and $25 from his sister. "You don't understand Greeks."

Through him I had met Gerard Malanga, a poet who was Andy
Warhol's right-hand man. And there was P. Adams Sitney, a wisp of a guy
with much knowledge of underground films. And Jonas Mekas of An-
thology Film Archives, with whom Gregory later had a bitter feud. For
Mekas and for Gregory, avant-garde films were "like bread, music, trees,
or steel bridges." In brief, they were everyday life.

To Gregory Markopoulos, the movie projector was the machine of
desires. 11th Street was making me dizzy. My host introduced me to
Anais Nin, she of the notorious journals. Anais Nin invited me to her
place at six o'clock precisely.

I was doubly thrilled. I'll be fed, I'll bet, a delicious Greek repast
and perhaps I'll end up in her journal. Her place was smaller than Gregory's
though filled with elegant objects.

Meanwhile, my tummy rumbled.

"Come in." She got down to business instantly. "Move my televi-
sion," she pointed. "Over there." I grunted and moved the piece of furni-

ture on which it rested, and set the TV in place. She gave me a glass of water. "Thank you," she said. Showing me the door. I went to a market and bought some crackers.

Oh. Louise remembered my birthday, April Fool's Day.

I was thrilled by that.

11 May 1962

Dear Jan

Are you still mad at me? You would forgive yourself if you could see your green pitcher filled with purple lilacs.

And may I say something about my hard words to you and others. Just once, to be kind, I said I like a person's work which was bad. Later he came to see that it was bad too, and he has thought me a fool ever since.

The MAD AT BROOKS CLUB is a seething kettle.

My sister is sore because I wrote that her dream of her husband becoming a Catholic and giving up Wenching, Drinking and Gambling would never come true.

Glennon had to be told that he couldn't come up. A difficult letter. I love Glennon. On the phone he told me that he had been given a grand Farewell party—they are tearing down his building—at the New York A.C. The Lord Mayor of Dublin, Driscoe, was the guest of honor. Dinner coats all round—and when Paul turned up in his twisted old trench coat, Dennis (the little fat bar tender) had to be physically restrained from throwing Paul out one of the French windows on 59th Street.

I wrote Henri that his rosy exaggerations of his power in being able to make Eastman House bigger than the Museum of Modern Art was doomed. "When the General died, Kodak deliberately left his baby to suffocate in the fearful, jealous grasp of his nurse maids." And that his faith in Jimmie's upholding him in FIAT was an illusion.

To Maas, about his writing I wrote that I liked his style but "There is something about it that makes me think of a man belching after an excellent dinner he ate 30 years ago."

Maas is okay. He had the guts in his piece in this months FILMWISE to call Dick Griffith the rat he is, sighting chapter and verse.

When Griffith and Card are together their likeness is striking. People are mislead by the petty jealousy they display to protect themselves from light striking the film people who do not grasp that Card and Griffith are a team employed in the business of killing private possession, private showing, and private circulation of films.

How dense these kids are I did not realize—the outsiders—till I read Kenneth Anger's name as a Film Maker. I couldn't believe that anyone—simply because he cut an old dead pansy studio costume department worker's name off a title sheet and substituted his own—that anyone approaching sanity would make a picture STARRING—SERIOUSLY—a pitiful old Queen. Other than the old Queen himself. It is self-evident. And Kenneth, who was 27 in 1958, in his bit in PLEASURE DOME, has scarcely grown whiskers. But then I didn't believe either that anyone would print his picture book. A bunch of old dead photographs. A lot of ridiculous mumbo junk. A bunch of old dead gossip collected from make-up men and hair dressers. The lovers of filth are the dupes of liars.

Henri saw him in Hollywood and Kenneth sold him a sport coat "worn by Jimmie Dean."

I have heard the first two — Marion Davies — of my radio series. As always, the first exposure pleased me. The second made me sad. As always, as I say about everything I do…"Silly." Once I laughed and that was good.

Father Cousineau sent me OBJECTIV 62 from Montreal with a translation of Card's *S&S* article on me. Father says, "I like the French better. It depicts your present relationship with God filled with joy deepening and broadening." This would sadden Jimmie who worked so hard to make me desperate—phony suicide stuff and "the lower East Side." Gerald Pratley is coming down again to do a story on me for FILMS AND FILMING.

Father is coming down for the week-end of filming on the 31. Good old Jimmie is sailing May 26 for a "vacation" in Europe. Just about the time Langlois's estranged FIAF is meeting in Rome. So I will be on hand for my darling priest and his "large delegation." And right now I am going out to buy some clothes if I can find any to please me. All the junk here is the same in every store. If I had some dough I would go to New York and buy some decent rags. I have lost weight.

I was thinking. There are rooms to rent all round here. I am only a block from the University. If you liked you could come for a visit. My new cook book has inspired me. No, I don't suppose it's a good idea.

Love
Louise

Maas = Willard Maas, husband I think, to Marie Menken, both undergrounders who were among Gregory's circle of film folk. All with giant egos.

One I could tolerate more was Francis Thompson. In 1957 he made an inventive surreal color short, *N.Y., N. Y.,* in which through camera distortion the city floats, spins. NYC dances. His reputation is deserved.

Daily and punctually, Francis would dine at the same establishment run by a Miss Bell who perched on a chair near the cash-box mending bleached tablecloths. And every time he ordered her $2.85 extravaganza, tiny lambchops in delicate tutus of starched paper. I marveled at how he looked forward to them each night.

Ah, Kenneth Anger. With *Scorpio Rising* and *Inauguration of the Pleasure Dome* he became a bad boy, the Mick Jagger of the Underground. To Jonas Mekas, his films are perfect.

To me, occasional images are arresting. He is no Markopoulos. Or James Bidgood. Nor is he a lucid thinker. "...On the unspooling reel of Time, neither the Past, the Present nor the Future exist NOW; and if it is impossible to prove that any one of them *did* exist or *will* exist, then it cannot be proved that Time itself has *any existence* whatsoever."

These guys are so full of themselves.

In 1975 Anger published the trashy exposé *Hollywood Babylon*.

When I was in high school I wrote to Salvador Dali. What is the meaning of your LE CHIEN ANDALOU? His answer: "Nothing in the film signifies anything. DALI." I like the honesty.

Louise's birthday mass worked its magic. A contract was to be made up but why did it take so long? The novel now a distant matter.

Ursula Nordstrom showed off a flimsy nothing by Captain Kangaroo. Sendak was to illustrate... She made a boast, "THIS will sell. It will pay for yours." I wasn't sure, did she mean the *Wars* story or *Pleasant Fieldmouse?* Turned out to be *Fieldmouse.* Sendak would do the honors. He's smart as a whip, loves Wagner, thinks Walt Disney a bad man and must be punished. Now I suppose Maurice and I are friends but in New York one never knows.

Contract with Harper is big time! Sendak the best. Without asking Candida, I figure it's an advance of $10,000.

I hear of an established author who'll be in Europe for two years; wants to sublet a floor-through in Brooklyn Heights, 11 Cranberry Street. Fully furnished. With garden. Same address that'll be used in *Moonstruck* with Cher and, yes, Olympia Dukakis. A dandy historical district. Across from the Esplanade lies Wall Street lit up after dark with a shimmering presence. The next two streets are Pineapple and Orange. I'm not kidding. I move in.

1963

1963

7 N Goodman St
Rochester 7 NY
5 January 1963

Jan……

Your letter did not arrive till long after the Madonna. I was mixed up in a fight to get Card to return my stills. And I will talk about you after I tell you about the stills because it concerns everyone interested in the care and the seeing of films and the use of stills, etc.

Eight years ago Card as a representative of E. H. took all my stills—Pandora, Diary, French, and rare private and German photos. Never did he lend them to anyone. He hid them. Except his article *S&S.*

After months OBJECTIVE wrote Newhall asking why Card had not answered about borrowing my stills. Newhall forced Card to return the stills to me—not all—some of the rarest not.

He told Newhall I gave them to him "personally." He then pulled my confessor Fr Atwell into the mess giving them back through Fr Atwell. This great mess he made to discourage me from demanding the rest of my stills from him. And I'll bet he has copies of those he returned.

I know of many people who have given Card films and stills with no written record, for E. H. No titles, nothing saying they were given to E. H. Beaumont should listen.

When he (Card) declared that he would "obliterate" my films and stills he meant it, and he will, just as he did those stills of mine. Since everybody eventually becomes his enemy—Obliteration for all.

So precious few came back. For the Objectif magazine I hate to send them to Montreal after so much grief and 8 years of 'obliteration.' *How much does it cost to have copies made? Who can do it in Rochester? Please write me this, Jan.* I should have enough copies made so that I will not have to worry about the originals.

Newhall made Card send this apology along with the salvaged stills...."Dear Louise, You know perhaps better than anyone else that anger and vindictiveness stand near the top of the too long list of my weaknesses. I am ashamed that both were brought to bear in my harsh letter to you. I beg of you to forgive me. I sincerely hope that this new year will bring you the peace you seek and the *happy resolution of whatever it is that's troubling you.* Faithfully, Jim." The last line obviates any meaning in the sickening crap that went before.

And now to you, Jan. Your future looks bright in a world in which my mind is so dimly lighted. And I know you don't want Card platitudes from me. I'll say a prayer every morning to my Crystal Madonna for you. I am re-reading PICKWICK PAPERS and when I analize the wonders of genius—just in choosing a tense—I say I know nothing of writing. Just get what you want in your deals—look at the pushing around I have taken from Card because I would not take charge of myself and go to battle with his manipula-

Lulu in widow's weeds. *Pandora's Box* (1929).

tions of me like a can of film in his "private Collection" at Eastman House.

And experience shows this—that no matter how badly you handle yourself—other people will handle you a great deal worse and despise you in the bargain. So don't trust anybody's beautiful nature or promises outside your contract. And cover every outlet from Disney to the Comics.

That "Class" story about Rogers is sad because if she hadn't had her Ma around Astaire would have "obliterated" her because of her lack of class. He screamed it from the beginning with her—she didn't have class, he wanted a girl with class—a young Gertrude Lawrence. And when you have to work with a guy who walks away in contempt after every scene it's tough. But she ain't got class.

Glennon is working as a bar tender at his friend's saloon—Devlin's, 1649 Second Ave (about 90th). Go in to see him. He doesn't see many of the old gang. But when I talk to him on the phone he is still as sharp as a persimmon. He has to work or go mad. Every night, every day in the week with the privilege of taking off bang whenever and as long as he likes.

DIDN'T YOU GET THE FUDGE I SENT?

Love
Brooksie

Don't become too much of a Card to answer letters.

If we communicated by phone, there were fewer letters. We could afford to speak for just three minutes; big loss. On the other hand, I was able to listen to that musical voice.

Bus trips to Rochester. So I stayed at the Treadway, found out how to copy pictures, avoided Jim Card and Eastman House. If we watched movies they were of the "art" variety. Ingmar Bergman, re-issues of Mae West, W. C. Fields, Dietrich at the Little Theater run by a swell couple, the Belinsons.

Louise had a peculiar nose: if any patron of the movie house suffered from body odor, she sensed it and screamed with gusto.

Crash to earth.

My advance from Harper? *$500.* After I collapsed they upped it to one thousand.

I skedaddled to a cellar abode located at 140 Columbia Heights in a brownstone situated between Norman Mailer and Forrest-and-Wright who did musicals "Kismet" and "Song of Norway." My land countess suggested I appear promptly at 9:15 a.m. On the next morning when I moved in I knew why, for that is when the sun drifted down into the barred, opaque windows. An alcove with hot plate and baby fridge, midget bathroom, a gloomy room at $175 per month.

That left $20 a week for food & fun. For 365 days I did a kind of variation on Francis Thompson. Spaghetti with Campbell's tomato soup for sauce became the repast. And pancakes the second year, third year spaghetti.

The "Class" story was as follows:

Through Sendak I met a talented song writer unable to sell his songs: a protegé of Carl Van Vechten and other venerable celebrities. His name was Karel.

Ginger Rogers was to arrive at his studio to hear potential ditties for her cabaret gigs. Karel put me in the clothes-closet, door ajar so I might peek out and observe.

Ginger showed up, a veritable powdered and painted peacock hen. Karel tickled the ivories, introducing number after number. Ginger mulled each one over, tapped her fingers on his piano lid, pondering. "It's nice," she hedged. "But I need something with more, uh, class." A variation: "Don't you have something classier?" It went on and on like that until both were worn to a frazzle.

I had to tell Louise about it. To me, in *Top Hat* both Fred and Ginger are classy. I realize art is illusion.

Scott Schutte collection.

1964

7 N Goodman Street
Rochester 7 NY
13 May 1964

Dear Jan

VANITY FAIR came the 7. How dear of you. It is one of the few books I want to keep forever. In itself, I do not believe there has ever been a more nearly perfect book written. And such a nice edition. You are a tender flower, and I can use a bit of sweetness, as you shall hear…

PLEASANT FIELDMOUSE came the 8. It was a surprise. I expected something tough and garish. Like comic books, I guess, for I have not seen a children's book for years. The text is most imaginative and for action—great. The drawings are wonderful. Full of things to look at a long time. It is certainly a complete success, Jan's first book.

UNPLEASANT BROOKMOUSE'S PICNIK

As you know, ever since Frs Cousineau and Godin met Card and me in Toronto in 1957 they have been bringing a group down every Ascension Day week-end to look

PLEASANT
FIELDMOUSE

by JAN WAHL

pictures by
MAURICE SENDAK

at films at E. H. Now, Godin, bathed in his glory and
perfection, has never had sense enough to be a hypocrite.
Pushing people around in Montreal has been taken as a
God-given right by priests for so long that they really think
they *are* God. (Now, I see why they hate L'AGE D'OR—
it makes fun of such priests.)

When I wrote Cousineau last Christmas that I was finished with Card, I knew our friendship was ended. He never said a word about my being right about my photos or Card's blackmailing attempt. The implication being that I was a liar and crazy. But I had to get the full treatment, so I asked them to lunch on last Saturday.

Now, there is another plot running parallel with the Card plot. A bunch of kids have a magazine in Montreal – OBJECTIF. When they were down with Fr Poopfox and Fr Stinkowl last year they taped a long interview for their magazine which made the priests sore. In two issues I have appeared, not allowing Fr Poopfox to edit my material in French. I go along with some gags but the word censorship brings out the dragon in me. Now too, I sent the magazine to Wanger, Weinberg, Friede, etc, and they loved it—no holds barred.

I had been preparing my Picnic since dawn. Frs Poopfox and Stinkowl appear good and late with cold ugly faces.

They have had a talk with Cardass.

We sit down to chicken soup, steaks, etc....

Fr S: You shouldn't have fixed all this—no potatoes, Please!

Fr P: No, really (drawing back as if from merde)...You *know* we never eat lunch!

B: (Full in Fr P's puss) Then why did you *come* to lunch? (They are about to rise and leave but remember all the lunches I have watched them eat and make religious passes over the food in case it is poison.)

B: So you have seen Card?

Fr F: Yes, he spoke of you...wondered why you hadn't been around Eastman House lately...

B: He dared say that to you knowing that I have written you all about our fight—and
you said NOTHING?

Fr F: Well….

B: He had you just where he wants you, Father. He is a true scoundrel. Why did you not take my advice, when he did not answer your letters, and write Newhall? I tell you he means to cut you off entirely, like everyone else. Langlois never answered your letters or sent the films he promised. You had to phone Card at the last minute to come down, and half the pictures you wanted to see have been returned to the Museum of Modern Art. Why is that?

Fr F: Jim told me that Cinematheque and E H have broken off affiliations with the Museum of Modern Art.

B: You don't seem to remember anything I have written to you, but in December I wrote Dick Griffith that Langlois was telling everyone that "Langlois has been offered Griffith's job at the Museum."

B: (After a long sour priestly silence)
Have some French Bread – the boys, Andre and Pierre brought it form Montreal.

Fr S: No, really…(The two priests push back their full plates with distaste. I take them away.)

B: I don't suppose you want chocolate pie, or coffee—the boys brought the coffee (Joke) from Montreal too.

Frs P & S: Just a small piece. (They gobble up the pie, having made their point.)

B: You know, Andre only got my photos for OBJECTIF by writing Newhall, and Last night Card had LULU run for a small group of them….

Fr. P: (With a sneer of quite laughable innocence, waving it off the map) We have seen that picture twice….

B: Also, as you know, the last time Andre and Pierre came to look at films, Card got "sick" and wouldn't show them. Now, fearing that Andre would write Kodak, he has given them a date July 1.

Fr S: (Bristling with rage) He is making a great mistake—
Fr P: (With some plot already in mind) Yes, we will see—
it isn't July yet...

  After these kindly priests left and Unpleasant Brookmouse cleaned up the mess, she went to the store for some sauce. When Andre, Marie, Pierre and Jean-Pierre arrived at 5:30 they found B in a state of mental confusion. They had *told* me. And I had found *out*. So, Unpleasant Brookmouse, feeling her insomnia coming on, went to sleep. And next morning everything was eaten and drunk and clean and there was a note saying "We love you." So Unpleasant Brookmouse found that after all, her picnik had been a great success.

Love
Louise

Pleasant Fieldmouse was a hit with Louise.
Much relief.
Wanger = Walter Wanger, talent finder for Paramount, later important producer, husband of Joan Bennett.
Weinberg = Herman Weinberg, film buff, subtitle maker for foreign films in the 40's and 50's; made a poetic experimental "poem" *Autumn Fire* in 1931; another print Card never returned. Herman had the habit of rendering "all right" as "alright," even in the beautiful French classic *Devil in the Flesh*.
Friede = Donald Friede, co-owner in the 20's and 30's of Covici-Friede, a prestigious publishing house.
  The main portion of Louise's epistle is a wild take-off on a chapter from my storybook, in which the Fieldmouse decides to hold a picnic. I quote:

It was the beginning of May. The weather was neither too hot nor too cold.

"In fact, it is pleasant," he decided, hopping eagerly onto shore, where on the sand he sat, and with a sharp stick drew up plans.

"I'll invite only *good* people, because they don't cause trouble. There is always somebody you want to avoid. If everybody comes, you don't enjoy yourself, I do believe." Then he sighed, because it was a very sad truth.

Pleasant was more than happy putting up signs.

Therefore he made a fine set of them.

INVITED
GOOD PEEPLE (ONLY)
TO A PICNIK
MEET BY THE BLACKBERRY SWAMP
BUT STAY AWAY
TERIBLE OWL + TIRED FOX
& OTHERS LIKE YOO!

> TOOZ
> DAY

The upshot is his friends stay away.

Each of the forest folk finds defects in himself or herself and so believes he or she is unworthy. P. F. takes a nap, waiting for the guests. When he awakens, insects have devoured the feast.

"It must have been a stupendous picnic," he says. "Everything is licked clean."

7 N Goodman Street
Rochester 7 NY
22 May 1964

Dear Jan

I have torn up two long letters to you explaining that I wrote you to Brooklyn May 13 saying that I received VANITY FAIR May 7, and MOUSE, May 8.

If this letter doesn't get off, good-by! That is why I can't get started on NAKED. I have to re-read and re-write, and I can't go back. Looking at old films, reading odd stuff, all fills me with sorrow, without reference to good or bad.

But you know the OLD WOMAN wouldn't forget her bad Brat in his first triumph after years of struggle. And what success! First Class! Delightful writing, fine printing, and those wonderful drawings by Sendak.

And starring in your 1955 summer black suit. It isn't where or why or to whom you appear that makes it a moment of delight. It is your own feeling of accomplishment. And you should be proud of your work. Anyone who thinks writing for kids is kid's stuff, should try it. The problem of vocabulary alone would stop me. But I am glad to see you are not afraid of new words. When we are young, the most fascinating part of a book is the mystery of words. It was years before I found out that Tunken Tell was not Williams's brother. (More than tongue can tell)

Right now I am whipping through Fiedler's LOVE AND DEATH IN THE AMERICAN NOVEL. I hate it although I agree with everything he says, but it takes him 800 pages to say it. And I should thank him for making clear to me why I also hate American classics, those hideous homosexual pranks disguised in Hemingway whiskers.

But he never gets to the root of things. GATSBY, he says is Fitzgerald's best book. This, because of its orderliness. But contrary to all the vanities of non-geniuses, (nonegeniuses) nobody ever invents a real character. What is wrong from the depths of Gatsby is that Fitzgerald is pretending to be a bootlegger is 100% false. There were a few nice American boys turned bootlegger and I knew one intimately, Jimmie Mulcahy. Home and Mother and the Catholic Church and marrying a nice girl went hand in hand with the mob and the constant fear of death which never colored Gatsby.

How can anybody go to school to such guys as Fiedler and listen over and over to their few insights? And I thought I suffered when I listened to Joe Schenk tell the story of RESURRECTION. You, at least, had Nabakov, and Fiedler brushes him off as a guide book.

What interests me is Lord Alfred Douglas's MY FRIENDSHIP WITH OSCAR WILDE which I finally wrested (a limited edition) from the library. First, it is not about Oscar at all. Al whips through Oscar in no time. What it is about is his death feud with Robert Ross. Now, I have read seven different stories of what happened to the original letter (De Profundis) written by Wilde to Douglas. It is impossible not to believe Douglas on this point. When Oscar gave it to Ross to send to Douglas, Ross didn't. For such a vicious person as Douglas to hold his tongue about such a vicious letter would be impossible. And aren't the English incomparable? Ross gave the MS to the British Museum and Douglas could never get it back—his own letter, written to him, stolen by Ross.

It is also odd that the book is so terribly written and untouched by the editor and so becomes in a way a work of art. For it is written like a series of conversations in which the writer says over and over, like in talk, what he has said before, but each time adding new facts and thoughts and arguments. But the best argument Douglas has is his photograph. He was beautiful. Like all beauty, marred. The loose cruel and careless mouth.

Did I tell you that I got letters from all over about the two issues of OBJECTIF, the Montreal film magazine written by my young friends Andre, Pierre, and Jean-Pierre. They left my Filmography—Positive and Negative, just as I wrote it. And they wrote up a long tape just as I said it. It was this that showed me what rats Frs Cousineau and Godin were. They came to lunch, May 9, 1964, when Fr Cousineau went into a long scandalous tale about Beatrice Couve de Murville being the mistress of Langlois, I was finished. For I had written Cous that Beatrice was the daughter of the French Foreign Minister, that she was coming to "work" at Eastman House. And Cousineau knew that Henri was a homo besides having already, Mary Meerson for a mistress. But because they wanted to look at films here, they would whitewash Card, and make a fool of Langois. And me. Fuck them.

Love
Louise

Once again, your book is divine – and Vanity Fair a Treasure –

Vanity Fair is not the magazine but Thackeray's novel, which I found in a marvelous near-mint old edition. I felt Becky Sharp, sharp of tongue, was *the* heroine for Louise.

Impossible to take Thackeray's flavor off the page. But Rouben Mamoulian's bold 1935 Technicolor attempt (using the three-strip color vividly, particularly in the Ball Scene by increasing the red hue through-out, suggests the blood-bath happening off-camera at Waterloo) gives a good account of itself.

Miriam Hopkins with wicked bravado had the time of her life. No wonder this trenchant version is *Becky Sharp*. In her own way, Louise Brooks was a new Becky Sharp.

My first book was off and running. When I hoped the editor, Ursula Nordstrom, might give a slight hint of praise, her response was: "I must like it. I bought it." As I passed a row of desks Barbara Lucas whispered, "We think it is a classic."

The copy editor, Alice Kenner, taught me that the blue pencil is a mighty tool. Thanks to her, forty-five years later the book is still in print. The Captain Kangaroo book vanished.

Louise understands the mystery of words for children and the problem of the written word. To a child, learning to read, it's like going into one of those authentic cafes in Chinatown where colored flags hang on the wall—the menu printed in strange characters.

Those flags on the wall—do they proclaim "moo goo gai pan" or "1,000 year old duck eggs"? Those chicken scratches mean something, and must be learned.

Joe Schenck was a top producer from silent days on to Marilyn Monroe; in fact at age eighty he was powerful enough to make her briefly his girlfriend. *Resurrection* was a 1927 production starring Dolores Del Rio.

Louise looked bitterly upon imperfect priests.

7 North Goodman Street
Rochester 7 New York
14 July 1964

Dear Jan
　　What a cunning idea, your envelope, although I don't think it real darling—Pleasant Fieldmouse taking a swat at Unpleasant Brookmouse.

What the Mirror? item can be I do not know – but having worked for Winchell and knowing how "possible" items are invented — It is probably a concoction of my down-the-incinerator WOMEN IN FILMS and the yet unreleased compilation THE LOVE GODDESSES.

In a letter written jul 16 from John Springer (who does publicity for Dietrich, Garland, Burton, etc), he writes..."I've seen THE LOVE GODDESSES. The short but exciting sequence of you is undoubtedly one of the high spots of the picture. The producers of it are wooing me to get Richard Burton to narrate. Since Elizabeth is so importantly involved in it, he might just do it."

My God, have you read that vile HARLOW book? I heard the writer, Shulman, defending it, for 5 hours on the WOR Long John show, with phoney Freudian assumptions. Poor little Paul Bern, the complete masochist, accused of beating Jean so that she died 5 years later of euremia. Donald Friede (he is now with Doubleday) writes that he knew Jean "very well" in the last seven months of her life … and can "vouch for acres of what cannot even charitably be called errors in the pages dealing with that period." He is sending me the book. Apparently Shulman waited till Jean's mother died to write this slime, but Paul has 800 living relatives and I hope they sue the shit out of him.

Then have you read A MOVEABLE FEAST? Hemingway now really did write as he says – building line up on line, with perfection. But what a cruel, vain, humorless man he was. As Fitzgerald wrote, "Ernest is just as crazy, in another way, as I am." After 30 years, chewing up Stein and Fitzgerald till the gore of unabated hatred and envy runs down his chin.

That is what I found out about being able to write truth *only* in fiction. In a biography you start telling lies to fill in the gaps. In an autobiography you have to make everybody else a sonofabitch in order to justify yourself.

Springer also wrote... "I am thrilled about Walter Wanger and Donald Friede and your book... In your letters, I've appreciated your talents as a writer... it should be one of the most exciting book events... Then watch Card and Langois come jumping back to share the glory." (As if I would even fart on those two blubber heads.)

But it does make me laugh to think how Langlois will be oozing around Wanger when he gives him that projected Homage in the fall, oozing and prying to find out if I told Walter about the $196 still owed me on my plane ticket for the Homage given *me*. In 1958.

When the boys from Montreal were here in June I learned that Card has chopped LULU and DIARY to nubs on "moral" grounds, and that the rest of my films were "unavailable." I was curious to see how he would carry out my "oblivion," still keeping undercover.

As you know, Langlois was already thrown out of the European Archives. So now from Montreal I get a bulletin saying that Guy Cote (another prize ass-hole), president of the Canadian Cinematheque, "pointed out" that it was "a member of the Union Mondiale des Musees de Cinema, whose president is James Card, and whose Secretary-General is Henri Langlois." These windbags full of nothing but empty highsounding words... How I long for their collapse. What a terrible hater I am—without remission.

But I am also an enduring lover of 40 years – without remission. Hearing again that George Marshall was dying I wrote him last week saying I loved him. Yesterday came a letter from his assistant to the Redskins. A real man-to-man letter that made me feel like an old half-back, saying that George loved my letter, telling me to write more, and explaining that George had a stroke last July, that he is in Georgetown and, although he has constant nursing, he gets down to the office twice a week. You cannot imagine how full of joy and relief that makes me.

Weinberg sent me a translation from the Lusanne Congress 1963...It goes on and on in a rave notice that makes me feel sad — such a waste – 30 years too late. "The oldtimers have sung the praises of Louise Brooks with such verve that it is not without apprehension we have been waiting for her appearance. They were right. Long live Louise Brooks!! The most seductive smile in the history of cinema! We discovered a Louise Brooks of rare beauty, of an extraordinary cinematographic presence, who played with rare simplicity the upsetting young girl, with far more tanlent and naturalness than our present Brigitte Bardot. The technique throughout is dazzling."

Thirty years ago I allowed the critics to break my heart, saying I did not "act" – I did not "do anything," because I did not mug in the conventions of the period. If I am now "ageless," it is because I found such antics ludicrous without beauty, and played all my parts as ballets.

If you are going to stay put, I'll make you fudge some cool day. I hope to heaven you make a deal with Scribner's. They are much more your kind of publisher than anyone else you have tried. Anyhow, you sound gay and optimistic, and I feel that now you are off the ground with Fieldmouse, everything is going to be roses.

Love
Brookmouse

Oh, Louise. By her own admission she's a first class hater.

The Bastille Day letter demonstrates a remarkable love/hate thing she had about men. With Langlois, with Card, with George Marshall (not the director, the owner of the Washington Redskins). Only G. W. Pabst remains the adored one; he made her truly immortal.

What would have happened to me had I indulged in her preposterous notion for me to disguise myself as a girl and live under the same roof with her. I can't begin to imagine.

I never knew her brother Ted or sister June to visit. To them—was she a curiosity? The untamable black sheep? A thorn in their sides? They probably wished she had never made movies.

But they are gone and she lives as long as movies are preserved.

(handwritten in colored pencils)

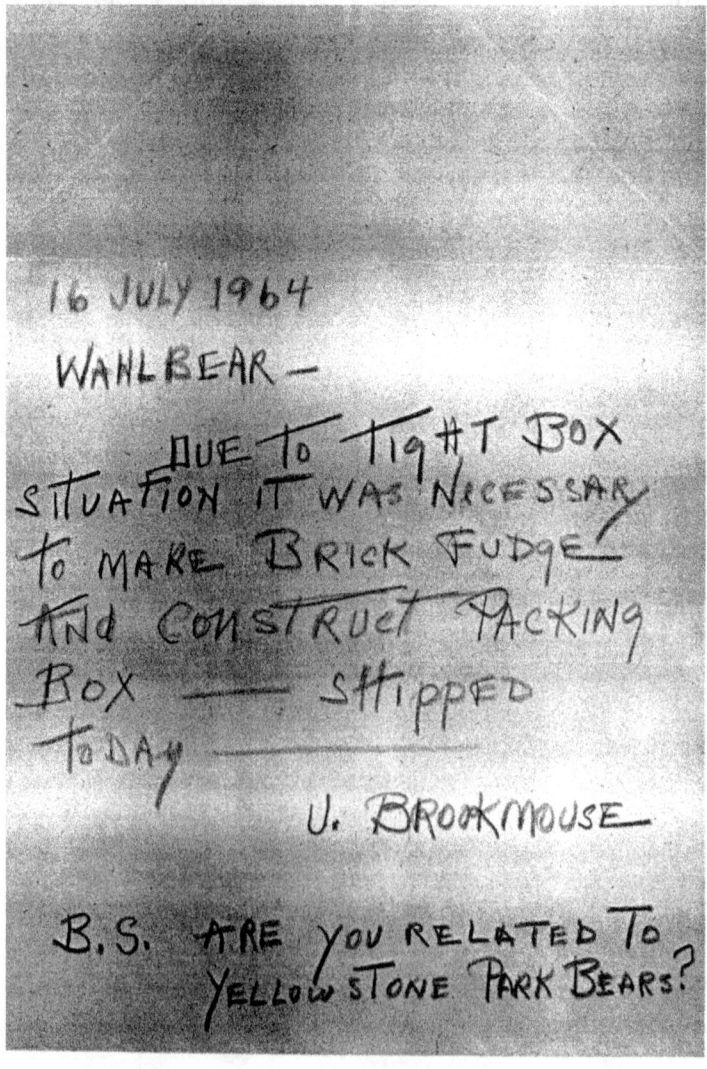

16 July 1964
WAHLBEAR –

Due to tight box situation it was necessary to make brick fudge and construct packing box ——shipped—— today

U. Brookmouse

B.S. Are you related to Yellowstone Park Bears?

7 North Goodman Street
Rochester 7 New York
6 August 1964

Dear Jan

The Beast Book is beautiful and lovely title. The drawings are like the Chinese, you feel the weight of their lying down.

And all your captions are perfect…Gorilla, goodbye… Children are full of sadness for all the beauty they see destroyed about them, and their own too.

Again I say, you are going first class. Brave competition with the Super Markets.

But your last letter is glum again. Even with the fine reviews of PLEASANT FIELDMOUSE you sent me. What you lack is a group of friends to keep you alive to yourself and your work important while you live through the unknown stage. New York is terrible that way. I remember those last years of mine, 1945-53, at 1075 First Avenue when I was looked down upon as a foreigner by the shopkeepers – Irish Italian. It was all I could do not to storm and rage at them – I am SOMEBODY! But it is no use. And you must curl up like an egg in a shell. Don't read the papers too much. Don't think of other people and get envious. How quickly their day passes.

Oh, I must tell you. I got an invitation to Jacob's Pillow, the 50th, the Golden Wedding day of Miss Ruth and Mr Shawn – of course they have been separated since 1930. But I could not resist the answer I sent (enclosed) to their request for "a message to be put in an album for Mr and Mrs Shawn."

I have been burning for 40 years (1924) because in 10 books, 1,000 articles and interviews and lectures, neither of them ever whispered my name. They were both wild to do pictures. And Carol Dempster and I have been given the silent treatment. In 1926 when I was making pictures at Paramount in Long Island, I went to Mr Shawn's classes just once. He began giving an imitation of my arabesque – lifting his leg like a dog at a tree which rather stunned the other pupils. Then when I got Card to copy his dance film free, Shawn made some sneaky reference to my name not being mentioned in his last really awful book – THOUSAND AND ONE NIGHTS. How do such terribly written books get published?

No, you can't tell a book by samplings. You can tell what you like. The Shulman book is full of truth. The episodes in San Francisco, San Bernadino, Mayer's beach house, could come right out of my book. Everyone hates it, not because it smears an actress, which is traditional, but because it tells some exact truth about L B Mayer and Paul Bern. Funny thing, for years I have wondered why Paul give me RUDYARD KIPLING'S VERSE for Christmas 1927 – like me sending you the collected verse of Edgar Guest, and in HARLOW I was made aware that Paul's "culture" was not so deep as a well. Because, you know then in 1925 when I went into pictures, I took it for granted that everybody read Proust and heard "The Ring."

So I am writing an article that came out of HARLOW. Shulman with his second-hand Jean also tells that second, third, fourth-hand story about John Gilbert's voice being lousy. A perfectly simple lie manufactured with the twist of the sound engineer's wrist. But everyone longed to believe it. All research shows the despicable desire to believe the worst of every lovely person. So I have done HARLOW RECALLS ANOTHER VOICE FROM THE DEAD. Ripping through the tricks played on Harlow, Clara Bow, and Gilbert. But my favorite paragraph....

I tell about a visit to Mayer's beach house with Peggy Fears, the.....

Nevertheless, the central incidents of his book are stunning with the shock of truth. Such scenes as the one at Louis B Mayer's beach house where he offers Jean the mink coat in exchange for her body should rip many pages of sentimental hypocracy and phony idol-worship out of future works on Hollywood. Infinitely more captivating to me that Shulman's murder by a dead man is his dead Harlow's laughter. In an article in a 1955 WOMAN'S HOME COMPANION, Joan Crawford, speaking of *Mr* Louis B Mayer, says, "He is honest, and doesn't play games." And "to this day I stand in his presence."

Louise

Ken Russell, who does the Monitor shows on BBC wants to do one on me, but I have written him that Card and Langlois will make my films hard to get. You might write him that you have a copy of PRIX DE BEAUTE.

Keith Lampe: "self portrait," Copenhagen

In 1964 I had four books published.

Harper and Holt both vying to be first to publish me. Yippee. Three books were picture books.

A writer is fond of throwing in lots of detail to give verisimilitude. A picture book text is more like making delicate haiku—each word precisely chosen. Not so easy.

How the Children Stopped the Wars, however, was still on hold. But Sendak promised to do it so I got the usual token $300. That was ten $3 dinners at the Red Brick, a modest Swedish restaurant where Garbo in-frequently dined. At least I had ten chances to see her.

The ghost of Viet Nam hovered close. Before the horrible assassina-tions of the two Kennedys, I telephoned, on behalf of the "Yippees," Robert. I was given his number by Jeannette Michael Haien, the concert pianist who taught me Harmony.

My idea: there might be a Christmas truce as did occur once during WWI. Kennedy listened. And snapped, "Listen, kid! The ONLY thing on my mind is going skiing."

Nevertheless, my friend Keith and I were elated; there was a kind of truce that Christmas.

Now the Shulman book is full of truth. Before, he was unfair about Paul Bern, but this time she had read the book. Her displeasure with Ted Shawn and Miss Ruth is explained: they never once mentioned her in all those years.

Amazing. In the same troupe had been Louise, Martha Graham, Carol Dempster.

7 North Goodman Street
Rochester 7 NY
24 August 1964

Dear Jan

You howl like a composite Wagner-Proust. I thought by this time you would have become some old man's dar-ling, living in a charming 19th century apartment with but-toned down plush, Modigliani, and Gide.

Or some nice, artistic broad? But you are too "moody." That was really what made you and Card enemies. You both got mad and sulked and went to bed at the same time. No-body could win.

If only I were thirty, in Hollywood, no, New York at 425 Park Avenue – torn down for an office building at 56th – you could live with me, wander in and out at will with nothing asked but talk of books – Russian, dancing – Graham, and how to open a bottle of hot champagne. I had sublet the apartment from a grand dame of Tuxedo who was always popping in on me unexpectedly to see what orgies actresses were up to. And as luck would have it she always found me in the sitting room, lined with book shelves filled with her husband's first editions of Wilde and Beardsley, reading Tolstoy. After a cup of tea brought in by my slovenly Irish maid, Rose, she would depart, bracing herself for a better attack.

No wonder I can't cook. In those days I only went into the kitchen to see what Peppy was howling about on her diet. 5' 5" – 180 lbs. All day she would starve at Mr Hearst's Warwick Hotel because Mr Hearst and Marion didn't give her any spending money for girls, and then she would bound in upon me, ordering all sorts of expensive liquors from "21" to be charged to George Marshall (it was prohibition). Then would appear Damita or other objects of her affection with some of my boys and we would play bridge or just fight after which Pepi would throw her tired body upon any thing in the ice box and then upon Mrs Jones' chaste Chinese bed in the room with blue Chinese damask silk walls. In the morning, Pepi would wake, screaming, "Rose," being herself half Irish and half Jewish that slut Rose could not put her down. And after rose's breakfast of plenty scrambled eggs and gins, Pepi would get on the phone to coo in lovely Jewish to her little girl friends that she was really Joe Schenck who wanted to give them a contract with MGM.

That is the life I wish you could have lived with me, carefree and gay, until you become famous and rich, which you shall

Love
Louise

Check for $10 enclosed————

The imaginary life Louise sketched for me was a nightmare. True, I was not living a glamorous life, not on $20 per week. Royalties would trickle in the next year. My books sold for $2.95, $2.95, $1.95 and $2.50, of which I was to receive 5%.

My land countess, Mrs. Othmer, also loved to come in snooping. Without knocking. Mostly to discover if I swept or dusted.

"Pepi" (a.k.a. Peppy) Lederer was the niece of Marion Davies; like Louise, high-spirited. And killed herself when she was twenty-five.

Somehow I met—oh yes, through Clay Lancaster of Lexington, Kentucky—Aunt Helen Fay, who lived upstate with three other older "girls." Aunt Helen was associated with luminaries such as Katherine Cornell and Ruth Gordon. I was impressed. Miss Cornell, grande dame of American theater, was to record *Pleasant Fieldmouse* for Caedmon Records—unfortunately succumbing to cancer before it happened.

Helen Fay shared a whopper of a tale about royalties.

It went like this: There was a lady of a certain age who wrote greeting cards for P. F. Volland and Company, esteemed publisher of Johnny Gruelle's *Raggedy Ann and Andy* stories and the masterful Frederick Richardson *Mother Goose*. First editions of the books, circa 1920, are superbly printed—using up to seventeen color plates.

But the royalty receiver in question composed greeting cards for which there was no public clamor (e.g., Washington's birthday). Like most authors she was convinced she was being cheated.

On a spring morning she took the train to Joliet, Illinois, where the publisher was located. She demanded to see Mr. P.F. Volland himself. The obliging gentleman emerged, to shake her hand. She pulled out a dainty silver pistol. Shooting him through the heart.

Louise had sent me a $10 check; I was to get giddy with it. I rushed to the Fillmore where Virgil Fox, the organist, played while a rainbow of lights flooded the auditorium to the delight of enthusiastic flower children.

7 N Goodman Street
Rochester 7 NY
28 August 1964

Dear Jan

You must get away from the lower classes. It is like bad writing, you can't be a journalist and say some day you will write well, because you have grown into a shell that won't let you write well.

Now, I have the perfect person for you to meet, Steve Wiman. I think she will ask you up once just to pick your brains about me, and then she will like you and have you around for all the things you like. But you mustn't be afraid of her like Card. I took him to see her and he froze into his Frog Footman roll and disgraced me.

She is about 70. She was married to Dwight Wiman – Deere & Co, Moline, Ill. – who produced all those divine shows – beginning with THE LITTLE SHOW. But I do not think she likes to talk about Dwight. In the end they hated each other and she called him a weak little pansy drunk — she hates drunks.

She had 4 daughters, Anna is dead from falling down stairs on her head in Bermuda. She is stingy. But in the freeloading department firstclass, and you can go to the opera. Still, I knew her only as a woman during her *any-*thing days. Now, I think she is quite pure. But she can be fun and she has lots of amusing people around her.

Through her, you could meet lots of attractive people, and through her daughters and their friends, young people who would do you good.

All you have to do is be like you were when I met you in Copenhagen, show your teeth, and look beautiful, and tell her all your troubles, she is a voracious liver of other people's lives.

Please do not show this letter to your friends. I give you this rundown for your private use.

So dream up a note to send along after the copy of this note I give you. Say that you don't know what to do but obey my orders.....

I am glad you were able to celebrate THE BEAST BOOK. Your friend has been sent the autographed photo, and thanks for Bette Davis.

Love
Louise

I am also sending Steve the Chicago Tribute notice you just sent me.

Mrs Stephen Wiman, 800 Park Avenue, New York 21, New York

7 North Goodman Street
Rochester 7 New York
28 August 1964

Dear Steve

I have a darling friend, a beautiful boy (30) who is trying to make it the hard way.

He has published two children's books but his curious novel, DANCING ON THE SAND, has been going the rounds with no takers – yet.

Jan comes from a good Toledo, Ohio family and he went to Cornell, so I am not promoting another clown.

It is just that he writes me from Brooklyn about the simply dreadful people he is thrown with… "Painters living in lousy lofts, psychologists with babies and pretty wives, leaning left.."

And I thought maybe you would ask him to one of your wonderful fish luncheons....he was in Copenhagen on a Fullbright grant.

I have asked him to write you a note. If you want to see him, okay. If not, nothing is lost.

It is terrible to see beautiful, talented people go down the drain for lack of other beautiful people to cheer them on. He will be just as surprised as you to get a copy of this note. What made me think that you could advise him well was that you and Jan are the only people who have ever called me "Brooks."

Love
Brooks

(handwritten)

Jan —if you do not hear from Steve at once — she is often away on trips ——

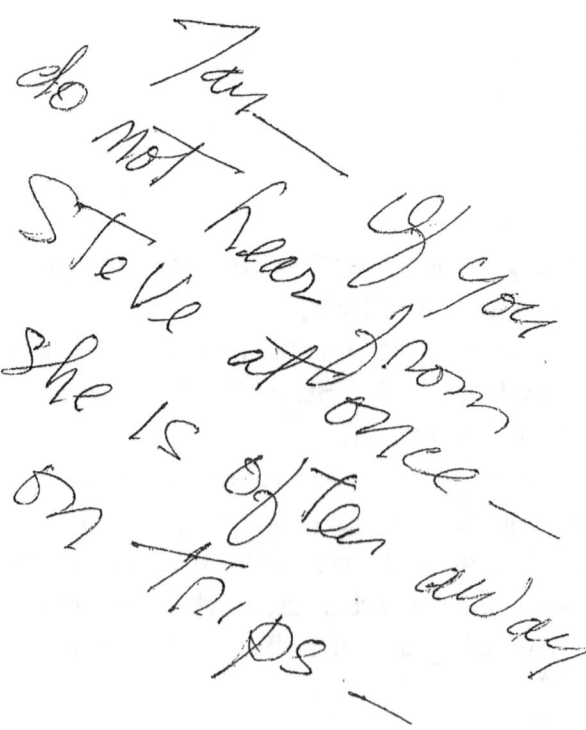

I didn't hanker to be a Park Avenue woman's darling. Did I really describe people I knew as "leaning left"? Whew.

On the whole, my books won good reviews from the *New York Times, Chicago Tribune, Boston Globe,* etc.: "Irresistible," "A barrel of fun," "Wit, humor and delightful logic," "Young readers will be enchanted," "Warm, imaginative story," "Most beguiling book," "Plu-Perfect!"

The Howards Go Sledding is a family of guinea pigs; Mr. and Mrs. Howard and the children Bumps and Teeny attempt to deliver a birthday cake for Aunt Hilda. Alas, they suppose they can do it sledding down a hill with no snow. *Go Sledding* sold at the same price as *Fieldmouse.* Holt put it on the cover of their little catalog.

I was spending countless hours on stories that won't change the world.

I was obsessed with bringing the carnage in Viet Nam to an end. Accordingly I carried a sign, NO MORE WAR, and in the process got pelted with eggs or beer bottles. I was not fond of Abbie Hoffman; I admired Jerry Rubin. The cops particularly around the United Nations were nasty and I learned to duck and run.

Why wasn't Sendak equally concerned? When was he going to do the *Wars* book?

7 N Goodman
Rochester 7 NY
20 September 1964

Dear Jan

How do you stand this writing business? I sent P Houston my article (17 pages – 4300 carefully chosen words), "*HARLOW* RECALLS JOHN GILBERT'S VOICE FROM THE DEAD," and got the following reply.

SIGHT AND SOUND 16 September 1964

Dear Miss Brooks,

Very many thanks for your letter and for the sensational article. Of course, I'm immensely glad to have it and very gratified that SIGHT AND SOUND is the magazine you thought of first.

As previously you have set us something of a legal problem and I imagine that any British libel expect is going to be horrified by some of your allegations against the companies – particularly MGM who have a great record for bringing legal actions. I think the best thing we can do is to get a legal opinion as soon as possible, modify or cut where we have to, and then send you the revised version to see how you feel about it. Let's hope that we can get away at least with most of it.

Yours, sincerely,
Penelope Houston

++++++++++++++ ++++ ++++++++++++++

What disgusts me is that I researched my research and my life to get exact facts. And then I cut the re-write so that every word would hang together to make a picture from which the reader could draw his own conclusions. If Houston cuts names and re-writes, all the clews will be lost. Thinking of libel I make all my points with quotes from HOLLYWOOD RAJAH, HARLOW, or Photoplay. Published material. I never say Garbo is a dyke or that MGM pitched Gilbert's voice up to a squeal.

Did you get in contact with Steve Wiman? Or is she out of town somewhere warming her old bones on the beach?

Thanks for the St Denis, Shawn publicity. They are remarkable. I have known people to be madly in love with themselves periodically, but Ted and Ruth have made careers of it.

If I leave Rochester it won't be because of the Frog Footman, but the Public Library. I got LADY CHATTERLY'S LOVER out of the vaults and found pages torn out. All this sex reading is for my book, and the way I feel now, it won't be written. Chatterly is a work of art, sad, beautiful, and all of the autobiographical novels I have read, the only one in which the hero didn't give me a pain in the arse. Now, I want to read TROPIC OF CANCER. Your friend, Don Smith, wrote me a sweet letter. Thank him for me. He said he could get books for me. Can he send me Cancer and the Chaplin book? And anything else. I am desperate. I brought home from the Wellknown library three Samuel Beckett books. Half the words I cannot pronounce, never heard of, and don't know the meaning of. A second string Joyce, he leaves me bitched, buggered and bewildered.

What has happened to your novel? Friede is still on my tail, but after the reception of *HARLOW*, a true story from her agent who loved her madly, I think I'll give up. As you know I do not write about pricks and tits, but I seem to make men much madder with laughter. As Lawrence wrote – it is that kind of sexual shame that ruins all sex which is not a sentimental experience. Still, even Lawrence has his taboos, what he calls Lesbian love making (the fool), aggressive female love making. Having explored the field to my complete satisfaction, it comes to this. The most depraved person approves only of his own kind of sex, and finds everything else horrid, nasty, disgusting. Like a famous buggerer of little boys I knew who couldn't bear to sit near a woman when she was menstruating.

Come to think of it, Harlow was innocence itself compared to Carol Lombard who was happily and completely depraved with no shame and no feat – and nobody ever attached her with junk. Some of the parlour games her little group went in for make HARLOW dainty reading. No doubt now that the bars are down, somebody will write the Lombard book.

> Love
> Brooks

I'll bet Louise could show Ove Brusendorff a few fine tricks. D. H. Lawrence, too.

Through Aunt Helen Fay I met a real sweetheart, Margaret Hamilton, and was invited with her to a home-cooked meal at the Hamilton flat on Gramercy Park.

I was in awe to find, in the crowded living room, sitting in a chair quite blotto, Herbert Marshall; in another, ditto, Shirley Temple's screen daddy James Dunn; working her way through the crowd a short pudgy lady, Enid Markey, "Jane" of the first celluloid *Tarzan of the Apes* (1918—her "Tarzan" was a hefty Elmo Lincoln).

I was delighted to encounter the fluttery actress Dorothy Stickney, whose husband Howard wrote *Life with Father*. Miss Stickney plays "Miss Bird" in one of my top movies and Martin Scorsese's favorite, *The Uninvited*, the best ghost movie ever. "Nobody remembers I was in it," she said, with a wan smile.

Our gracious hostess was tickled to hear I was from Ohio. She informed me she'd been a kindergarten teacher in Cleveland before heading with her small son in a jalopy for the orange groves of sunny California. My head swam from blueberry wine and knowing I was elbow to elbow with historical personages.

Mrs. Wiman couldn't equal this.

I was caught by Miss Hamilton stuffing delectable oatmeal muffins in my pockets for breakfast. She gave a nod—suggesting approval. The Wicked Witch would have blasted me with a wave of her wand!

7 N Goodman
Rochester 7 NY
21 September 1964

Dear Jan

I hate people who send documents bare. So I will go on with my troubles. How do I get into them? I got out of my financial mess, I got out of my Catholic mess, I got out of my Card mess – and now I enslave myself with a book....Here is Donald Friede's last letter –

September 18
DOUBLEDAY

Dear Louise

I am *furious* that I missed you on the telephone the other day. I could have been reached so easily at another number that I am doubly furious. All I was doing was sitting at the Alonquin while MacKinlay Kantor was reading me wonderful pages from his new book. Did you call me on something specific, or was it just because you were in town? Or did you call me from Rochester? I am most anxious to hear from you because I think the time has come – as I have said before – for me to see something. What that something is doesn't matter in the least. It can be anything from any part of the book. But it will give me an idea of what I will have to work on with you. I repeat that I/we am/are very much interested in your book, and that I want to PROCEED. Do let me hear from you.

Love,

Donald

I called him from Rochester to call the whole deal off. If Houston calls my mildest work "sensational," I hate to think what my autobiography would be called. And Friede wants not a novel but an autobiography which would probably kill off George Marshall, and Peggy Fears would poison me.

Friede thought HARLOW was *frightful* three months ago when he sent it to me and I raved about it. But since then, as I said it would, it has gone to be top seller and two movies are in the making.

Now, I would hold out for a novel, but my first draft shows me I do not know my trade – to have 40 imaginary characters photographed on my memory without great experience is like – IMPOSSIBLE! Two years of work which I would love. But you see, I have been trapped again, hustled, yanked around from the outside, out of the Catholic frying pan and the Frog-Footman into the Friede.

You know all about this racket. Would you settle for a dodged up autobiography and loot? I can send him the Harlow, Bow, Gilbert, Garbo piece S&S is publishing.

Or say NO———?

Love
Brooks

(SHE ADDS POSTSCRIPTS:)

The dialogue in Beckett is marvelous —— Dylan Thomas must have thought so too.

Would you like Fudge Wahlbear?

———L. Brookmouse ———

So, according to Louise Brookmouse, Beckett is no longer second-rate James Joyce. Like many of us he gets a reprieve.

On the face of it, her long-time acquaintance Donald Friede (and with Doubleday to publish) would be a plus for an editor. However, most likely she could not bear to be judged by a friend.

In New York there are ways to get around not spending money. I managed to get into the old Met free—the Metropolitan Opera of the purple velvet curtains. Isadora danced on that stage. If you knew one of the ticket takers, you handed him a piece of colored cardboard same size as the ticket. He would tell you, "Box so and so, seat so and so," and in you went. Otherwise it was standing room at the back.

I saw Rise Stevens do one of her last "Carmen" appearances. She wore a lot-cut, seductive Spanish tight bodice. Singing a very forceful high note, both nipples sprang out. A delicious surprise.

Without missing a beat, she made a 360 degree turn and, still singing, snapped them back into place.

Standing room went wild but we in the boxes managed, just managed, to exhibit decorum.

Maria Callas doing "Tosca" could not match this sublime moment.

7 North Goodman Street
Rochester 7 NY
7 October 1964

Dear Jan

Don't read those bum reviews, especially when the broad doesn't even know who wrote the book. And you see what they mean. Everybody either panned HARLOW or gave it a light brush. It is at the top of the best seller list. I am re-reading TOM JONES—magnificent—and Fielding puts critics where they belong – it is just a racket, with rare exceptions.

Well, you made up my mind for me. My book must be an auto-biog.

Enclosed is a note I got from Steve yesterday with your letter.

Perhaps I described her in a way to frighten you. Everybody is a different person with everybody else. And although Steve and I had many reasons to be leary of each other, I feel that you were made for each other. With her help you can get the kind of attention that brings success. She is a power house. It never did please me, your chasing around after people to print your books. Outside of running her apartment, the servants, her kids and grandchildren, she has nothing to put her mind to. And I have one of my hunches that she would love to help you.

Anyhow, isn't if fun to have a try from the lap of luxury in which you fit so gracefully? I wouldn't stick my neck out with either you or Steve unless I believed that. Card taught me a great lesson. You can't put a smelly hick who acts like a discharged butler in that world.

Write her a little note to Newport and ask whether you can call when she gets back to town. Don't be ashamed of your address. That will mean nothing to her.

Love

I thought your friend *Don* was going to send me some books.

Brooks

Scott Schutte collection.

Don = Don Smith, buyer for books at the late B. Altman on 34th Street.

Hope he liked the autographed photo.

Lap of Luxury? Not my goal. It was to get *How the Children Stopped the Wars* published.

On Columbia Heights I had difficulty falling asleep. The New York headquarters for Jehovah Witnesses lay in one direction, a hospital in the other. People kept passing by talking loudly, sometimes someone called for help. Fully dressed, I sprang to the rescue.

A woman was screaming. A man holding a broken bottle was about to attack. With as much force as I could muster I kicked him hard on the tailbone. She screamed at me: "Will you stay out of this?"

Another woman yelled. She came to retrieve her parked car to find a young man in the act of breaking a rear window and taking her TV from the back seat. A police car stopped. The policeman asked for her name and address.

"No, look!" she wailed. *"There he goes!"* The robber carrying the TV zipped around the corner to disappear in the subway entrance below the St. George Hotel.

Without turning his head the officer continued to inquire as to her address.

About four a.m. was the last cry for help, a happy lull and I could sleep.

7 North Goodman Street
Rochester 7 NY
7 October 1964

Dear Jan

Your letter to Steve is fine. It is the most impossible kind of letter to write.

Now, I have another idea. Why don't you sell her on the idea of doing *a picture book on Dwight* with your script?
THE THEATRE OF DWIGHT DEERE WIMAN

Steve Wiman and Jan Wahl

It seems to me she would have a lot of fun getting together and selecting photographs and documents. And it makes me furious to hear people talk about the great show men and leave Dwight out. Tell her it's my idea – So you won't be pushy and scheming –

His shows were always original, new, full of taste and class and glamour. THE LITTLE SHOWS – Rodgers and Hart, Libby Holman, Clifton Webb, Fred Allen. The first play Fred Astaire did without Adele – THE GAY DIVORCE that put him in pictures. ON YOUR SHOES, Zorina, Murder on Tenth Avenue, Ray Bolger. Many people became stars after his shows. And his last show, STREET SCENE, Kurt Weill. (Old man Brady and Alice....his beginning in the theatre)

Why don't you go to the Theatre department of the 42nd St library and mouse through his stuff? They must have a lot of pictures. And I don't remember half the lovely plays and musicals he did. Then you would have something to talk from – to Steve.

Houston turned down the HARLOW-Gilbert piece. "To quote our lawyer, 'It is of course impossible to write this story without defaming MGM. It may be true, but I doubt very much if it could nowadays be *proved* (for legal purposes, that is) to be true."

The Houston asked for an article on Pabst. So I sent her an outline for an okay – PABST AND LULU. I am not to be trusted in the material world. What seems to me perfectly "normal" can be quite horrid. I was so busy showing how MGM operated with their Black Book and blackmail that I didn't realize I was slandering my darling Garbo. Knowing how it would be after Houston's first letter, I had sent the script and a letter to Donald Friede saying that if he found HARLOW "disgusting" he would find my book disgusting. That I didn't want to harm anybody, slander anybody, and I would give up the book.

Just ten minutes ago the script came back special delivery with Donald's letter explaining that he found HARLOW disgusting because he and Harlow were going to get married in September 1937. It all hangs together. That summer she was talking about a book originating from her telephone book. And just to show you that my intuitions are always right here is a paragraph from my article.

Excerpt

"HARLOW" RECALLS JOHN GILBERT'S VOICE FROM THE DEAD

I met her just once. One night at the Cocoanut Grove all eyes turned to the top of the stairs at the entrance to behold a star. I looked too expecting to see somebody like Dietrich, sparkling in jewels and spangles. It was Harlow in her uniform, the white satin evening dress with a pair of net panties underneath. Nothing else. No jewelry, no handbag. Bill Powell was carrying her coat. She looked at me as if she had awakened in the night and come downstairs in her nightgown for a glass of milk.

She had a gallant air, following the headwaiter past the staring eyes to be seated at a table next to mine. After they were settled, Bill said hello to me and introduced Jean who leaned over, translucent, friendly and smiling with a nice purr in her voice like Jean Arthur's. *Later on in the evening I watched them talking together. They are not in love, I thought, there is no tension.*

****

Donald does admit that HARLOW gives the first true picture "of the utter rottenness of Hollywood." He says he can tell from my article that MY book wouldn't be "disgusting." ...."Are we together again?"...."Where do we go from here?"....

But he does not do anything to solve my real problem – the people I would hurt. Houston made me realize that people like Peggy Fears would be wild. And your suggestion about giving phoney names is an out, but no good. When I read blind Items, I put down the book.

When Houston spoke of the "Garbo references, which are equally dangerous if she wanted to sue us," I became sure that she is one of the girls. (I talked to her once on the phone from Paris to London.) So I warned her in my letter that I was going to libel myself because ever since LULU I have had an international reputation as a lesbian. People don't *ask*, they *tell* me. The point I am making is that the public in general and the people you know too believe you are what you play on the screen. If Garbo hadn't made CHRISTINA, the word would never have gotten spread around. And look at that busy little woman, Janet Gaynor? Yet who would believe that she isn't 100% SEVENTH HEAVEN?

Brooks

Lo these decades later, a tome about showman Dwight Wiman appeals mightily since the Twenties and Thirties and Forties were bright nights on Broadway. But I couldn't take time out to concentrate on the career of this remarkable fellow.

Today, a lavish coffee table book by Rizzoli or Abrams would be worthy tribute. Not nostalgia, rather a glimpse of riches lost.

Where did Steve Wiman's treasure trove of memorabilia go. Scattered to the winds?

I was riding high. I was compared to Beatrix Potter, A. A. Milne, Kenneth Graham, my masters. (They still are my masters.) There was generosity in reviews for kids' books; newspapers gave them space. Just before Christmas *The New Yorker* devoted twenty pages to new arrivals for the small set.

Holt asked a splendid artist, Adrienne Adams, to do my *Cabbage Moon*. She flew from the Virgin Islands and read the story, announcing, "I MUST do it, there's no reality here at all."

Harper signed up the illustrator of *Charlotte's Web* and *Stuart Little*, Garth Williams, for *Push Kitty*.

After Sendak elected not to do it, Harper had turned down *Cabbage Moon*; Ursula decided she hated it.

One evening in October I walked along the Brooklyn Heights esplanade with an English person, Barbara Dicks, who worked at Harper. A huge, round moon hung over the city, fantastic. "See? It is a cabbage!" said I.

Miss Dicks kept staring at her shoes as she stepped along, not interested. She wanted to see where she was going. "Moon, schmoon. I've seen the moon."

She was a New Yorker.

9 N Goodman Street
Rochester 7 NY
18 October 1964

Jan

Yes—I left the Church in the Spring. I told you.

I was an "intellectual" Catholic. I tried hard for 11 years, all the time observing myself and other Catholics. For myself, I found that it led often to great mistakes. For instance, trying to behave like a "Christian." Then I found that far from simplifying my problems, it increased them. Added to my personal pride and contempt and prejudices, it added those of the Church. Added to my natural ability to make enemies it augmented their hatred with people's hatred of Catholics.

The final joke was my having to make up a monthly confession to flatter my little pansy confessor who secretly feared and hated me because I knew his passion for his quite obvious homo boyfriend who worked on the paper.

Yet, I might have held out a little longer if I had not observed what it did to ordinary people. My sister has become an absolute tyrant and fool posing as self-appointed saint. And here I saw everyone treating me in the most patronizing way. The better Catholics people think they are the more intolerant and nastier they are to everyone else. Priests ridden with ambition and envy. Nuns filled with holy superiority. And in the end the whole Church is just another grand financial racket. My stupid sister, for their flattery gives away all her dough for the glory of Rome. But they had had their last buck from me. (Except for Christmas food baskets which I *know* feed the poor.)

My last disgust was the two priests from Montreal. One does not need to kneel in prayer at an altar and get the old Roman shake to become a narrow-minded bigot. And priests wanting to censure my writing! God damn them all. But I told you all this. What do you see, what are you thinking about when you read my letters? Other people understand

And just "realizing" Donald Friede. His ex-partner, Pascal Covici died October 14 and Donald's secretary wrote that he was badly broken up about it and gone to the country for a few days. But he seems to be positive that he can hornswaggle me out of a book — while the reading of my article has only increased his will to get it. (Personally, he is a sweet, sweet man.)

I just read GERALD by du Maurier. What a silly book from an established writer. The novelized biography is maddening. You never know what the hell is going on, not even when her father died. The Chaplin book is both good and bad. All that footage wasted to name drop, as if a great genius had need of a bunch of names to make himself great. And what he does say has been said. He even goes for old dead gags like that dead story about "all those lights hanging on buildings spelling Marion Davies"! People say Charlie is proud. He is humble. You see that whenever he talked about his work. He throws his genius away to write about Lady "Louis" Montbatten – Damn! (Lady Louise?)

The first thing I learned writing for Winchell was to send him only first-hand gags. As sure as somebody *gave* me a gag, he would return my copy with a notation…"Will Rogers said this in 1914."

I am delighted about your going to Toledo to ham it up and sign your name. Recognition will keep you going till the big break comes. And I am tickled about THE BEAST BOOK which deserves all praise and success.

What are you working on now? A novel I hope. I wrote Don Smith that Henry Miller left me cold because he writes like I talk. What people want is not to read shit and fuck that they live with, or how many fingers Henry Miller got up some girl's whatever which can interest nobody, but a true novel – a magic world of people living and talking and thinking and doing things that make us part of that world, saying yes and saying no, and laughing and crying.

The fact is that nobody can write a novel anymore. The concentration to keep that world of fiction going – plot and people – is beyond the powers of people today. Balzac, Proust, Dickens, Tolstoy, Fielding. Who can keep countless people moving in a great book today? Those people who might do it have turned to films.

You were a darling to run out for the FACT address. Herman Weinberg sent me a copy of the first issue. I don't think they would care for me and I know I don't care for them. Slander is not my object. Nor sensationalism. I was thinking of an article for ESQUIRE – COME-ON GIRL FOR WILSON

MIZNER. About the time I took Fred Levy with Wilson to a gambling house and Fred lost $2,000 at Black Jack while I sat innocently drinking champagne at the dice table and won $200. It was three years later when I was dancing at the Chez Paris (1934 AND GOT A NOTE FROM Fred Levy addressed to "The come-on girl for Wilson Mizner" that I understood the plot and Fred never believed that I was innocent.

It would be a most amusing piece on Wilson; and Grant Clarke (the son of writer of "Am I Blue?") who said all the things attributed to Wilson. "Hollywood is like riding through a sewer in a glass bottomed boat – one turd after another." "The trouble with Hollywood is that you are too degenerate for one group and not degenerated enough for the other." And sitting with Texas Guinan in the El Fay, unable to get a waiter. "Reach down in your heart, Texas, and get me a piece of cracked ice."

But then, like the HARLOW piece, I would probably discover that I had done some people a lot of harm. Because you know my articles cover a lot of people and incidents.

Yes, I am fearfully depressed. I love writing and can't please anybody. It is the truth that makes people fascinating and unique, and nobody wants it. As I wrote Houston …"Everybody in Paris is furious with me because I say Stroheim had *NO sex life* to speak of outside of the usual domestic fuck." And Houston is lesbian-conscious. And you are Isadora Duncan-conscious, hating my WORD AND MOVEMENT. And Friede is Harlow-conscious and Jewish producer-conscious. (As FACT would be.)

Strange, that I have never belonged to any group. The Catholics were leary of me too – and right they were. And when I made films it was the same except for Pabst. I don't belong anywhere, to anyone, to anything.

Love,
Brooks

(*Handwritten:*)

> I am sending the fudge to Don
> since you are away ──────

"I don't belong anywhere, to anyone, to anything." That last sentence sums up Louise's life in a nutshell. Devastating. Truly she felt alone.

I am certain it was Gregory Markopoulos who had sent Joseph Cornell to me on Columbia Heights, he of the collage boxes containing an array of found objects. In 1936 Cornell concocted a film, *Rose Hobart*. By taking an actual print of a film in which the actress appeared, he snipped it apart and re-assembled it, making a surreal new object as Gregory did on a larger scale in *Serenity*.

He was a skinny little rodent kind of fellow and slid into the doorway to sniff around the room until he happened upon the print of *Prix de Beauté* that Beaumont Newhall returned. He gazed off into the distance to say, "If you give me this you may have one of my boxes."

"No thanks," I replied and let him out and shut the gate behind him. I may as well have done it since I was to lose the print soon after.

If I had only known Jim Card had given him my precious 1902 hand-painted print of Loie Fuller, I would have thrown him out quicker. Did the little guy cut that 35mm one-of-a-kind? There is no movie of Nijinsky, there is none of Isadora.

The La Loie rarity to me is rarer than a box by that dismal twerp.

Brooks
N Goodman St
Rochester NY 14607

> Jan Wahl
> 140 Columbia Heights
> Brooklyn N. Y. 11201

BROOKS
7 N. Goodman St
Rochester NY 14607

Jan Wahl
140 Columbia Heights
Brooklyn N.Y. 11201

(*handwritten*) Christmas Card

Jan—

Steve's number is Lehigh 5 – 9252
Thanks for the *Beast* card.
Merry Christmas

Brooksie

(Handwritten) Christmas Card

Dear Brooks –

Your young man has not got in touch with Phyllis Facksore, the agent friend of mine — Why not? Tell him to come see me —-

Love

Steve

Very Best Wishes
for a
Merry Christmas
and a
Happy New Year

Steve Wiman

7 North Goodman Street
Rochester New York 14607
28 May 1965

Dear Jan

     Your CABBAGE MOON came this morning. To me
it is your best book for children. It excites wonder with the
enticing title, and things like the stilts which never quite
hang together – just like life.

     And the opening line is a darling … "Cabbage moon,
Jennie loves you."

     Also your Adrienne Adams is perfect for you. She
has form and movement and her colors are delightful, especially, her Van Gogh bedroom.

     With this book you seem to have found yourself for
sure. Freed yourself from the publishers' demand for
Disneyland

     Like Max Beerbohm and Roland Firbank, your seri-
ous novels will have to be found by some great critics. The
trouble is that in their time they could be published cheaply,

whereas now no publisher will take a chance on prestige works because of the expense.

Stay in there.....

Love
Louise

It was the era of "happenings." Swiss artist Jean Tingley blew up his own sculpture in MoMA's garden, a big signal event.

For $5, at a rented hall in the East Village you could stay as long as you wished, listening to a pianist play the identical note over and over and over. Then as soon as that pianist wearied, another took the same note with gusto.

When I paid my admission to a somber person dressed in black, a black tuxedo actually with a black shirt, there were only two girls there. I sat just behind. I had a hunch they'd been listening for hours; maybe they'll unlock the mystery. Finally one of them decided, "I'm starting to get it."

For $10, at an uptown gallery everything was cleared away and we breathlessly watched in a now-empty room, pressed tight against the walls, as two slim Asians in leotards appeared—tossing streamers in the air—at random.

The young man and woman went about their business as if this obliterated any other art. We watchers stood awe-struck.

After a nice review for *Cabbage Moon* in the *New York Times*, I went to Scribner's Book Store on Fifth Avenue. At the back of the store, Lavinia Russ, the buyer for the children's department, held up my book. She shouted, "Write another of these and I'll kill you!"

My next-door neighbor Norman Mailer continued to play the game of sticking his tongue out at me. I was the sissy kid writer, he was the tough guy.

One Sunday morning I came out to fetch the *Times* to discover a Cuban bantam-weight prize fighter lying on his doorstep. He had knocked him out and deposited him as a trophy.

One afternoon in Mailer's backyard he tussled with his pal, the actor Rip Torn. In a playful act he bit off Rip's ear. That didn't seem so terribly grown-up to me.

7 North Goodman Street
Rochester NY 14607
6 August 1965

Dear Jan

Hollis Alpert was here for a day last December taping me for Playboy. And you can find whiffs of me in Garbo, etc. Also I gave him the idea for the bosom lay-out of photos in the 1955 June issue. Like everyone who wasn't there, he thought it was a leg era – the 20's, until I explained that to Ziegfeld, George White and the Shuberts, beautiful breasts never went out of fashion and Billie Dove's were as famous in her time as Harlow's. Yes, I would like the Harlow novel – out of Donald Friede.

Donald is dead. He died a few months after I wrote up the most horrible chapter of NAKED ON MY GOAT as a short story and sent it to him. He was horrified. Now Mike Hall is determined to do something with it. Mike publicized Levine's *Harlow* which he called "soft."

He was the first admirer of my prose when we worked together for Ed Weiner, the publicist who worked for Walter Winchell. 1944.

Mike is thinking of NAKED as a movie, and let him play! But I want neither a publisher nor an agent. I am a loner. I danced alone and I acted alone and I will write alone. Penelope Houston is a perfect editor for me. Misspelling, libel, and a bunch of commas sprinkled around is about all I can stand

But that is because I am not writing for money. Yours is another problem and I am glad you have found a decent publisher in Seymour Lawrence. He is good if he believes in you *as you are.*

Nobody with a new viewpoint ever succeeded without a faithful impresario. And I see that I was wrong about Isadora because I judged her from her motherly photographs. And all the burlesques on her. Everybody I have read whose opinions I respect says that when she went into action she lifted you into a sublime sphere with her acting. You must read that dyke lover of Garbo's the direct descendent of the Duchess of Alba, Goya's mistress, Mercedes de Acosta's HERE LIES MY HEART. She tells how Isadora danced for her in a barn, humming note perfect a Beethoven symphony.

Bill Everson was here last weekend trying to see Card who was "on vacation." From Monday till Wednesday he was on the hunt. Lunching with me on Tuesday, he said that, since I could not see films with honor at Eastman House (although last month I looked at THE GRAND DUCHESS AND THE WAITER, LADY WINDEMERE'S FAN, and SHOULDER ARMS) he would mail up the Mal St Clair films, M. Verdoux and anything else I wanted to see in October. Fly up, rent a projector and run them for me. "Thank you, you are a darling," I said with the gay goodbys. Next morning when I woke up I said to myself, "My God, he meant that." I called him at the Treadway and he said, "Certainly, I meant it."

So come down for the screening. You can entertain his brilliant daughter who is six and speaks better English with more precision than I do. After having to sit still three hours looking at films, she was pretty wild when she got here and my tension about my lovely toys was noticeable.

Her paws were sticky with chocolate and peanuts and I couldn't bring myself to pull out your lovely books.

At lunch she announced that she drank coffee and she drank from a little Chinese cup I have without breaking it. She is most perfect in co-ordination. The pay-off was that I wrote Irene in Alexandria, NY who sent you the Chinese boy on bullock, to send Bandie Everson a $3 Chinese cup. If she breaks it I won't see.

To return to your writing. Stay crazy. When I read Hollis Alpert's description of me as "patent-leathery Louise Brooks," this cheap Time and Life writing about me, the only thing he could think to say after a day's talk, (for he has never seen one of my films or anybody else's he writes about), I am reminded of Agee who bragged about writing his reviews without seeing pictures. "Two friends of mine give opposing criticisms and out of them I write my reviews." He does/did/ not write about seeing, he wrote about words.

Love
Brooksie

Thanks for the tear sheets ——-

Thank God. I am vindicated about Isadora. Louise and I already agreed that Loie Fuller was important. Neither woman had what is considered the ideal dancer's figure for they had full womanly figures.

In fact "la Loie" (as the French termed her) was plump and not beautiful. Yet she was a revolutionary who mesmerized Toulouse-Lautrec and Sarah Bernhardt, just as Isadora was to fire up Rodin and Matisse.

Loie Fuller hailed from Chicago and was to win glory in Paris, dancing on a translucent (glass?) stage with ever-changing colored lamps below. She wore loose, flimsy, flowing long skirts with sticks sewn inside so that she could whirl her skirts about in all directions. With much skill

Loie Fuller, photo by Reutlinger, Paris, 1900. Jan Wahl collection.

she gave the effect of a rose unfolding or folding its gossamer petals, she could be an erotic flame or a magnificent butterfly beating its wings in air. Like Isadora, she drove audiences to a frenzy of ecstasy.

You don't have to have been there. Intelligent reviewers, drawings, photos give hints. But if there's a movie, that helps.

She influenced the art nouveau moment. She influenced René Clair who assisted her when she made an experimental fairytale feature *The Lily of Life* in 1920. She employed negative instead of positive film, she used slow motion, concentrated light sources, silhouettes, superimposition.

This was too revolutionary to pull multitudes into the theaters. She inspired Jean Cocteau later: those bare arms reaching out of the palace walls to hold lit torches in his *La Belle et La Bête* are right out of her movie.

Sarah Bernhardt beseeched la Loie to share her secret lighting effects. No wonder I was stunned when Card gave my precious Loie Fuller handpainted reel to Joseph Cornell. I had left it at Eastman House for safekeeping.

7 N Goodman St
Rocheste NY 14607
23 August 1965

Dear Jan

I didn't really believe that Bill Everson would go to the trouble and expense of bringing a bunch of films up here to run for me until he wrote, setting the date for the weekend of the 11 September.

Then it hit me! I simply couldn't allow such extravagance and work for absolutely nothing from me. So I wrote calling the whole business off, in case you were planning to come here. Maybe I can get up enough courage to get on a plane and go down to New York to see the Mal St. Clair films, etc at Bill's apartment.

In the September PLAYBOY (they sent me an advance issue) Hollis Alpert writes quite a bit about me and uses a lot of the material I gave him. He has just written me for a Garbo story for her 60 birthday Times story and I sent him a bit about Chaplin meeting Garbo. He said he would *quote* me. Then he asked me to write a letter to PLAYBOY on SEX IN CINEMA — "they like that sort of thing" — but there I draw the line. There is a John Springer and an Andrew Sarris letter in the September issue. Unless it is righting a wrong I think such letters are too silly for words.

From Vienna, Michael Pabst sent me some marvelous, unpublished stills from LULU, DIARY, etc. I was so delighted that I called G. W. Pabst Vienna, got Michael on the phone, and couldn't understand why he was so fuzzy. It cost me 12 bucks just to make him understand—Louise Brooks. Two days later I realized ten o'clock here was three in the morning there.

And Michael is sending me more pictures. Mr. Pabst has the finest collection of me in the world. In 1928 I gave him all the Paramount stills, never anticipating that I would some day write my little pieces and want them.

With this in mind I wrote Beaumont Newhall, saying that since Card swore that he returned all my stills; and those he hid in his house were no good to him or anybody else without producing them and proving, what everybody knows anyhow—that he is a liar and a thief, I proposed to give Card copies of the sex stills from Pabst if Card would copy my stills for his private collection and return my originals.

Don Smith wrote me one of his scrawls on 4 pound paper saying that he hated writing and what was my phone number. So I called *him* up at four in the morning and he sounds like a darling.

The telephone is the last of my expensive vices. I must take the cure. One call leads to another and a bigger one. I even tried to get Lotte on the phone in Paris, but thank God "nobody" is in Paris in August. Maybe Bill Paley will raise my allowance with all this inflation, or you will get rich with your lovely books and send me phone calls on a Wahl Elephant.

Love
Louise

Jan Wahl at Brooklyn Botanical Gardens. Photo by Herman Gustin.

William K. "Bill" Everson, an Englishman residing in the City, was *the* collector of collectors. He made film buffs such as Dan Bursik and me small potatoes. The wooden floors in his low-rent flat sagged from accumulated weight from stacks upon stacks of enticing metal cans with titles that made us drool with envy.

I had friendlier neighbors than Mr. Mailer. Over on Willow Street in a Federal-style gray house lived an old gent who was often at the curb washing his vintage Buick. I was told this was the composer of a popular ditty, "How Much Is That Doggy in the Window." Really? I had to test it.

Sauntering idly by as he washed his car, I whistled that tune. Instead of giving his usual nod or smile, he put down the hose. And grew reflective.

As if it were an electrifying idea, he said: "I am thinking of a new song…" He paused to give the moment its importance. "Something about a cat…."

Once I was invited to an open house party at Oliver Smith's, also on Willow. He was the set designer to Broadway plays. I walked from room to room admiring the fancy silk swags, the bric-a-brac, the tinkling chandeliers.

On a lower floor in an Edwardian parlor was an antique divan. One of the silk cushions had a message pinned on; the note warned:

PLEASE DO NOT SIT.
GRETA GARBO SAT
ON THIS CUSHION.

There was the imprint. A holy thing.

In the next room an elderly lady, in a fetching, lazy high-pitched Southern drawl, related a bawdy story. It was humorous, a genuine rib-tickler, yet shocking, coming from such a cultivated source.

I crept in. An enthusiastic group obstructed my view so I stood on tiptoe. The old lady lay upon a chaise lounge — sprawling gracefully, gesturing with little pink hands.

The old lady was Truman Capote.

7 North Goodman Street
Rochester NY 14607
25 October 1965

Dear Jan

Thank you for HELLO ELEPHANT. It looks like another winner.

From Michael Pabst I have just received 50 stills from DIARY, LULU, Paramount, and family pictures.

Good does come out of evil. If Card had not stolen my stills, I would never have thought of writing Mr Pabst for more.

And Michael gave me Dr Pines's address in Paris so that I can get stills from PRIX DE BEAUTE.

I have had a lot of visitors lately, John Besford from London, and Gerald Pratley and Andrew Sarris are coming up to see me in November.

Love
Louise

My new publisher, Seymour Lawrence, hoped to get mobile artist Alexander Calder to do *The Bird Book* in wire. A first! Calder was too ill.

For *Hello Elephant* at Holt I had England's premier illustrator, Edward Ardizzone. I was working with artists I loved since I was a child.

Soon I was to work with Feodor Rojankovsky. And with Norman Rockwell. Also my contemporaries, all rising stars: Uri Shulevitz, Fernando Krahn, Mercer Mayer, Steven Kellogg, Tomie di Paola.

Not to forget Edward Gorey, he of the tennis sneakers, fur jacket and byzantine rings; thus he was garbed as we strolled up Fifth Avenue on a hot summer day. Ted did *Cobweb Castle* and his kitties snoozed on his watercolors. So in Belgium, where the printing happened, fine white cat hairs got peeled off painstakingly with miniature tweezers.

After the grueling morning labors, the printers had more wine than lunch. So the afternoon results were fuzzy. Swiss publishers Diogenes had to go back to the artwork for "Schloss Spinnweb," now cat free.

I almost hooked up with Jacob Lawrence.

Grandma Moses. Robert Flaherty.

The plan was to use their work and deliver texts around it. Using photographs by Flaherty's widow, Frances, I was eager to make a black and white picture book out of the Sabu film *The Elephant Boy*.

If I could combine movies with my writing I would be in heaven.

At least, thanks to David Shepard, I had a memorable day with Frances Flaherty on her mountain in Vermont — the thin air made me feel I was floating. I was on top of the world.

1966

Letters from Louise for the entire year of 1966 are lost.

Visitors were flocking to Louise's door; recognition grew apace. What James Card and Henri Langlois had known—that hers was "the face of the century"—others were now acknowledging. 7 North Goodman became a kind of Mecca to many film buffs.

That was when Roddy McDowall moved into her heart; he came to photograph her for a book, *Double Exposure.* Observing that she did not possess a color TV, he pitched in with the Springer brothers, each contributing $100, to bestow upon her this luxury. Besides, Roddy was a film actor, active in the business she loved and loathed. They had much to share. He called her the "enigma."

She sent fudge; I sent my own books. I could not compete on his level. Time out for me.

Harper had suggested I travel down to Mexico to light fires under Garth Williams; he had not begun *Push Kitty.* He seemed to be on permanent vacation.

Famed for his drawings for Laura Ingalls Wilder and Margaret Wise Brown, the illustrator of *Charlotte's Web* was resting. When I got to Guanajuato in 1966 he told me, "No work between meals."

Garth married a beautiful country girl who knocked at the door, inquiring if he needed a maid. "Come in," he announced. "I need a

Photo by Roddy McDowall, Rochester, 1966.

wife." Alicia was a dear soul; she and I became friends instantly. Alicia had a son by Garth, Dylan. Dylan had her coloring, Garth's square Welsh head.

Garth awakened me at six one morning. "Get dressed quickly!" His father-in-law, his gardener, reported an accident on a mountain between Guanajuato and Marfil. A bus, Yellow Arrow, whose motto was

"Better Dead Than Late," had toppled off the road into a canyon. Was anyone alive? We observed boys with paint buckets and brushes below, painting the wreckage *blue*—the color of a rival bus line.

Mexico has its own realities. The mountain atmosphere was heady, produce in the market vibrant and ripe, the moon more immense than any moon in the States, strangers smiled at you, in the countryside you existed in the 17th century.

Guanajuato lay twenty minutes away. A pastel colonial city like structures imagined by Piranese, built between mountains over a river I was to call Rio Stinko. Spaniards settled because Guanajuato ("hill of frogs") had a huge silver deposit. I grew enamored of the twisty, narrow cobblestone streets and the tall gold-encrusted baroque churches—the

Jan Wahl, artist Guillermo Silva and family, Guanajuato. Photo by June Brown.

latter incongruous with so much poverty... Did New York exist?

I tried living one foot in each sphere, New York and Marfil; precarious. I met Harry Brown the novelist, poet and Academy Award-winning scriptwriter and his wife June, ex-Richard Avedon *Vogue* model; June acted as rental and purchase agent.

I would cross the Border, soon feel compelled to escape to this fantasy realm with such beauty and hardship. It seemed more real than what lay up North.

Perhaps I forgot to write Louise.

1967

7 North Goodman Street – Rochester NY 14607 –
27 October 1967

Dear Jan

Thank you for the beautiful book, POCAHONTAS
IN LONDON.
When I went back to Wichita in 1940 the only books
I had disappeared from among the thousands that filled
our house from cellar to attic were my children's books
My mother, who never pretended to give a damn
about her four unwanted brats, loved children's books and
loved to read out loud. I wonder now how she found such
expensive books, beautifully illustrated in color, in a little
Kansas prairie village like Cherryvale. My Hans Andersen
and Grimms' Fairy Tales bound in white calf with gold letters; my Alice in yellow cloth; my Child's Garden of Verses,
Oliver Twist, Little Women, Robinson Crusoe – Gulliver's
Travels – where are they now?
Best of all, I loved the wobbly red and green and
white MOTHER GOOSE made of cloth which my mother
read to us long after we could read for ourselves.

"Victuals and drink…" How deliciously mysterious. How deliciously mysterious the whole strange and English picture of life and nonsense.

Your POCAHONTAS captures that same mysteriousness that sets a child's imagination free.

++++++++++

Your script which used to be so neat has become less easy to read – is this part of your "facing yourself." If you are speaking of some sexual re-adjustment it doesn't appear very solid. How come you say nothing of your great love Greta or what has happened to her?

Why don't you do a portrait 'collage' of Asta Nielsen? I am sure Penelope Houston of Sight & Sound would take it and you could make yourself a fast $100. Nielsen's comment on Garbo is fascinating. (Mr Pabst had one hell of a time working with Nielsen after she realized Garbo had become the star of Joyless Street. And what did Nielsen think of me as Lulu – tell me – Gurrrrr!

Kevin Brownlow writes… "Already your piece on Pabst (PABST & LULU, S&S, Summer 1965) has become a much referred to classic here (London), constantly quoted in Film Society programme notes." Your Nielsen piece would be sensational.

Robert Benayoun's translation of my HUMPHREY AND BOGEY (Positif, February 1967: S&S, Winter 1966/ 67) was pretty ornate, but Denis Marion's translation of my ON LOCATION WITH BILLY WELLMAN, which Price of Secker & Warburg of London has just sent me, is tense and sharp. It is a young girl's story without self-pity or self-justification. On location with BEGGARS OF LIFE 1928 I went to bed with my double Harvey who asked me publicly next morning whether I had syphilis..."You know my job depends on my health – besides my girl is coming up to-day..."

Love   Louise

Louise's love for children's books is disarming. A revelation. She kept that part well hidden.

The difference between us was I must cultivate the child within. A writer for children has to see as a child does. Everything brand new.

As a small boy I only had two books. Both gems. *Little Pig Robinson* was one of Beatrix Potter's last tales; the image of hungry Little Pig

Jan Wahl bargaining in Oaxaca. Photo by Isaac Uribe.

Robinson in dinner-bib sticks in my brain. And the spectacular *The Knave of Hearts* by Louise Sanders, paintings by genius illustrator Maxfield Parrish.

I destroyed *Knave of Hearts*. An oversized book, and a rare item, it was about 11x13, an edition published by Scribner in 1925 with tissue paper between plates. Why this was entrusted to me I have no inkling. The depiction of Pastry Cooks Wielding Giant Spoons was so eerie it spooked me, caused me to feel insignificant. I grabbed the nearest crayon to deface the page. Into the wastebasket. What a blunder.

John Alcorn had a design studio, Push-Pin. Peter Max worked with him. John's artwork for our *Pocahontas* won us top prize at Bologna Book Fair.

Yes, why didn't I do a "collage" on divine Asta Nielsen (1881-1972). A true shining star. She gets several pages in *Through a Lens Darkly*.

Divine Asta, a.k.a. "The Tenth Muse," was adept at farce or tragedy as prostitute, ballet dancer, suffragette, gypsy girl, Spanish dancer or teenager. And she was *Hamlet,* she was Strindberg's *Miss Julie,* she was Ibsen's *Hedda Gabler.* She was *Lulu* in 1923. She was phenomenal.

When I knew her, I refrained from broaching the subject of Brooks's *Lulu* after she ripped apart her rival Greta Garbo. But Nielsen's version was by an equally super director, Leopold Jessner.

In 1996 MoMA screened its ASTA celebration from January 26 to March 15, with piano accompaniment by Stuart Oderman.

Louise's finely-honed pieces on Bogart, on Pabst and *Pandora's Box*, on William Wellman and *Beggars of Life*, are gathered in her ultimate book, *LULU in Hollywood.*

1968

7 North Goodman Street – Rochester NY 14607 –
13 April 1968

Dear Jan

You are the most astonishing boy. Just when I decide that I shall never hear from you again – only last Friday I made up a list of the enemies I have made since I met Card and got mixed up with the men occupied in turning their addiction to staring at old films into money – you send me a cunning red ducklett, beautifully packaged *air mail* you idiot:

Only you ever send me toys that please me. It is our common love of being ten and believing in fairy tales. Nobody ever comes into my apartment without a strange wondering look and a happy sense of release. They don't know why. They do not realize that they are returning to a child's world of order, form and color. Here is no pride in the past, no expensive competition — ugly old photographs, pretentious furniture. No, it is just like the little house I imagined as a child in Cherryvale when, in the back yard, I laid out red brick rooms arranged with broken bits of colored glass.

But I am an old woman who can play house on my idle way to death. You are a young man struggling for fame and fortune. It is time for you to put your toy life away and face your past and write it in a novel.

I have just been reading a great book on Dickens...THE MAKING OF CHARLES DICKENS by Christopher Hibbert who makes so clear that all Dickens ever wrote about was his life from birth 1812 to the death of his wife's sister 1837. I understand because my whole life has been a brooding over and an investigation into the experience that scared my soul up to the age of twenty-two. It is true of everyone.

Too late I took up the craft of writing. I am too old to learn the discipline of holding together a created world of people which is necessary for a novel. I do not care enough anymore because the fire of success burned out in me many years ago. But when you say the novel is dead you are only giving yourself an excuse for not undertaking a fearful task. A task which you are equipped to do by talent and training, lacking only the courage to look at yourself without tears or shame.

Love
Louise

Triumph! Louise and me on same page. Finally. A philosophical letter. Touched me deeply. In this one I can forgive anything.

She'd sent a letter I tore up. I gave her a book of mine of which I was proud as punch. Her response was "On the whole I prefer my old green-covered WIZARD OF OZ."

The summer of 1968 was meaningful world-wide—a watershed for me. Was I to remain in Mexico or keep the place I had moved to on Staten Island? Madam Othmer was too much.

One of my editors had dropped by with a girlfriend who happened to be a strong black woman. Remember when I peeked out as the song

Jan Wahl contemplating nature, Marfil. Photo by Armie Belloli.

writer tried his wares on Miss Ginger Rogers? None of them "classy" enough? That was Karel. The trio stood in the vestibule, knocking at my door. Ever-curious Madam Othmer sprang into the hall.

"I'd like you to meet my editor," I explained, nodding at the tall white woman. "And this is her roommate," without pointing at either of the other two. I let Mrs. O. sweat it out. Which was worse. Which was better. A strong-looking black woman or a guy with a prominent Jewish beak? She rolled her eyes in horror and fled.

Students were protesting the interference in Viet Nam. Vocally, physically, urgently. In Paris youngsters set automobiles afire. In this country demonstrations were peaceful. Yet at Kent State, our Ohio Guard met the challenge by killing students.

Just two years prior I was 1-A, after many student deferments. An 18-year-old sat on the waiting bench beside me. "What do you think of that nasty war?" I wondered. And his blue eyes twinkled. "Gotta lick them Commies!" he replied.

An angel of mercy sidled up. "Aren't you the nice boy who writes those books they sell at Lamson Bros. Store?" Humbly I confessed. The draft board lady quietly added, "You're too nice to go," and typed out a new card, 5-F or something similar and gave it to me. "Go, go, go."

My brother Rob was saved also, however Philip and Douglas and Michael and Douglas saw service and David later jumped out a window.

Having waited impatiently six years and counting, I knew Sendak washed his hands of *How the Children Stopped the Wars*. My then-agent insisted I return Harper's $300. No way. Farrar, Straus & Giroux offered a contract. Brilliant editing from Michael di Capua.

But I must support my belief with action. So — off to Chicago by bus for big protest march at the Democrats' convention. My usual sign, NO MORE WAR.

Chicago was my last encounter with Keith Lampe. A friendship blooming from Ann Arbor, transplanted to Copenhagen, carried to NYC and birth of the Yippees. At the convention Keith wore his Sgt. Pepper's uniform, looking impressive in it. Interviewed on TV, he declared this was the time to work from within. To infiltrate Wall Street and beyond. Which Jerry Rubin did.

Cops wielding clubs chased Keith who dashed off-camera for his life. Cops bashed my buddies' heads in, hurled bodies through plate-glass windows. I laid down my sign.

I'm a writer. Not a warrior. Where were Weronika and Steve? Were they in the thick of the fray as papier-mâché six-foot flowers?

Bus to Toledo. Plane down to Mexico.

Goodbye, U.S.A.

1969

7 North Goodman Street – Rochester NY 14607 –
18 April 1969

Dear Jan

Thank you for *May Horses.* Delcorte has done a lovely job. Do people really pay $5 for a sweet book to be torn and crayoned and stickied by little brats? Several years ago Bill Everson was here with his little girl five. I was too mean to produce your books for her to mess up. She was a pretty, intelligent child, turned into a monster of spoiled starring material. It is tragic when a man like Bill, with the appeal of a white enamel toilet seat, steals the scene by exploiting a child.

Blair Lent's drawings are full of the detail I liked to ponder as a child. The colors, with their dark brilliance, make me think of cyclone weather in Kansas.

Your script baffles me. How does a man pick out 650 words which will excite the imagination of a child? Evidently you know because you are so successful at this job. In one way I know you are right. You do not try to be funny. Children are serious.

===============================

On 4 March I went to make my will with my lawyer Harry Messina. When I got home I found a note from Allan Cusio enclosing a *New Yorker* article (22 February 1969) SHE WALKS IN BEAUTY by S J Perelman in which he spoke of me as "the immortal Louise Brooks."

I don't know Perelman but I couldn't resist writing him a note asking why he hadn't let me in on my immortality, saving me the trouble and expense of will-making. And what was I to do for a third act.

I send you a copy of his answering letter because it is so young. And he is 64. Perhaps that is the secret of happiness – not pretending to grow up, because we never do.

++++++++++++++++++++++++++++++

Have you seen the film ISADORA. Kevin Brownlow sent me the book from which it was made. Sewell Stokes' ISADORA first published in England in 1928. Stokes was a journalist who knew Duncan in her last years. It is the best book I have ever read about an actress. Like she is. What I have read about the film makes it sentimental crap. But perhaps the producers are right. SUNSET BOULEVARD, telling some truth about an actress, was a boxoffice failure. I'll see it when it gets here. Since I have stopped writing film articles I have time. I see films. I saw SHAME. Surely Bergman is the greatest director in the world today.

Love
Louise

S. J. Perelman, *The New Yorker* humorist and fan, replied to the letter Louise wrote on the day she made out her will. His was 10 April 1969:

"Your performance in pictures always gave me such pleasure, your vivacity and beauty were so exceptional, that they stamped themselves indelibly on my memory; and when, in writing that particular piece, I

Jan Wahl's "Mexican" godson, Jared Brown, Marfil. Photo by June Brown.

was trying to convey that special quality, my recollections of you return with great vividness. I hope this disclosure doesn't suffuse you with embarrassment. It shouldn't. I'd like you to believe that you created the same universal effect on my whole generation of moviegoers."

Indeed. Ray Bradbury swore that he, like many other boys and young men, succumbed to her charms. In reference to her last Will & Testament, Perelman stated it was invalid, "Since it has been firmly established that you're immortal."

She wasn't feeling immortal. Very severe arthritis was beginning to cripple already crippled fingers.

I had a slight connection with *The New Yorker.* In reviewing my book *Cobweb Castle*, Jean Stafford, one of the best adult authors around, called me "the incomparable."

This more than made up for a snide review I had from a contemporary, Jane Yolen, in the *N. Y. Times*, where she stated, "Jan Wahl always promises more than he delivers." I have not been given the chance to review one of her books.

1971

1971

No letters from Louise survive for 1970; during most of 1969 and some of 1970, again I was in Denmark.

(handwritten insert)

7 North Goodman
11 Jan 1971

Dear Jan

Many thanks for the *Wonderful Kite* – it's very pretty – My God – and you missed nothing – Alice, The Arabian Nights – "Little Master" TV, Maeterlinck, Swift ——-
I hope you've found your Blue Bird in Mexico – Although I agree with Colette – *Work* is the only happiness to be found in this life——-

Love
Louise

I forgot the *Tear* – Ste Thérèse and Mother Geneviève

217

7 North Goodman – 11 Jan 1971

Dear Jan –

Many thanks for the wonderful kite – it's very pretty – My God – and you missed nothing – Alice, the Arabian Nights – "Little Master" TV, Maeterlinck, Swift ———

I hope you've found your Blue Bird in Mexico – Although I agree with Colette – Work is the only happiness to be found in this life ———

Love

Louise

I forgot the Tear – Ste Thérèse and Mother Geneviève

Because of arthritis, Louise is no longer typewriting, and the letters are shorter; she must be saving her strength and energy for Kevin Brownlow, etc. The devil must have gotten into me for I made a reference to her once-admired St. Therese of Lieux.

The Wonderful Kite was my attempt to do an oriental magical tale. I had written it in Copenhagen, sitting in the King's park in Frederiksberg—near a Chinese bridge and pagoda. In olden days the King and Queen took tea there on summer afternoons.

My beloved Fru Halling told me, "Only when you finish, Jan, I tell you something." After I had finished she said: "That is the bench where Hans Andersen writes *Emperor's New Clothes*." A chill ran up and down me at that moment.

The Boston Globe was complimentary: "*The Wonderful Kite* bridges the gap between East and West in a way that no translation of Oriental folklore could. The flavor of the story is authentically Chinese, yet it communicates to us without the stiff quaintness of the Chinese folktale. (It) is in every way an extraordinary offering, one that could take its place on the permament shelf of fine literature for children."

Thank you.

I sat in my Mexican tropical garden reading Louise's reassuring note and looked up and was suddenly surprised by 10,000 white butterflies that flew down, quickly paused, then rose and continued on the quest of whatever it was they were seeking.

The invasion of butterflies and hearing good news from Lulu helped put NYC and book publishing in perspective. Here's a scene I reflected on:

> I'd been invited to a many-chambered apartment far up on Riverside Drive where a woman who lived with dozens of cats was holding a party. The household's felines were invisible that evening.
>
> Instead, the instant I entered I considered a line in W.C. Field's two-reeler for Mack Sennett, The Fatal Glass of Beer. Up in Alaska, where it isn't, according to him, "a fit night

Jan Wahl counting butterflies, Marfil. Photo by Armie Belloli.

*out for man or beast," he observes to his wife: "The ci-ity is
no place for women folk, but purty men go thar."*

*I wandered into the party and drifted through a swarm
of purty men. Ex-chorus boys? There was no liquor, in fact
no sustenance of any sort. But much light chatter about lost
loves, lost this, lost that. I was invisible too.*

*My waist then was a mere 32 inches yet I felt fat. I
sucked in my tummy and searched for the hostess. She sat,
wearing pretty pearls, in an overstuffed chair, and she wore
a fancy hat. She was a queen bee surrounded by honeybees.*

*There was a theme here but I was too dense to grasp it
until the door burst open. In came some older men easy to
identify. Bernstein the conductor, Gielgud the actor, Thomson
the composer. As if on a treasure hunt.*

*They happened to fix their steely gaze on me. And the
chase began. I climbed up on a sofa in the middle of the room
to escape. I leaped over its back, tumbled, scrambled to my feet
and fled.*

Ah. Better to count butterflies in Mexico.

Or to pick flowers.

When I arrived in Mexico City, from there I took a train to meet
Garth Williams, my illustrator for *Push Kitty*. It was summer, and the
rainy season caused this part of the country to burst into bloom.

The train rattled and shook and came into a valley filled with luxu-
rious flowers. The train, already an hour or so late, stopped on the tracks.
Many passengers, some of the crew and a few of the concessionaires
emerged—and all rushed into the landscape to gather the miraculous
bright colors. They really did.

It was a "happening" I will never forget. In America, I may have
been an ex-student and former flower child; here on one golden afternoon, I was among flower people.

The Show Off (1926). Scott Schutte collection.

1978

1978

(Handwritten)

19 September 1978

Dear Jan

Thanks for your *Youth's Magic Horn*. That's a handsome photo of you.

You must watch for Kenneth Tynan's *New Yorker Profile* of me which he is writing now along with robberies *in* Spain. Jaguar explosions and a hernia operation. He found Rochester repulsive so he is trying to lure me to Beverly Hills and his three lovely family for a visit and a "small party of 50 in your honor."

NO————-

Now that I can just walk with a cane because of hip arthritis, now that I am practically crazy, everyone finds me irresistible, wanting to drag me to festivals at Telluride, Chicago, Ontario, begging for my *Memoirs*, sending contracts for my collected articles film.

Ken is right about my picking a terrible ~~place~~ hole in which to die if I can get the pills.

> Love
> Louise

19 September 1978

Dear Jan — thanks for youthis magic thorn. That's a handsome photo of you.

You must watch for Kenneth Tynan's New Yorker Profile of me which he is writing now along with robberies in Spain, jaguar explosions and a hernia operation. He found Rochester repulsive so he is trying to lure me to Beverly Hills and his three lovely family for a visit and a "small party of 50 in your honor." No —

Now that I can just walk with a cane because of hip arthritis, now that I am practically crazy, everyone finds me irresistable, wanting to drag me to festivals at Telluride, chicago, Ontario, begging for my memoirs, sending contracts for my collected articles film.

hole Ken is right about my picking a terrible ~~place~~ in which to die if I can get the pills.

Love

Louise

In Mexico I was to be a party giver. Who better to throw parties for than Dolores Del Rio—gracious, diminutive, still gorgeous, patroness of the arts festival the Cervantina.

Burt Lancaster, trim and vigorous, dived into my pool as he had in *The Swimmer*, only to become violently ill from the polluted scummy water. Once a month Hilario left for Leon to buy chlorine, however apparently never using it.

Norman McLaren, sour and grumpy Canadian film-maker, visited once; he was not going to be my neighbor, I was happy to learn.

Youth's Magic Horn = my book of stories, dedicated to Louise with anticipation. What would she say? A reviewer wrote, "…as in the opening sentence of *At the Crossing*, he writes with something approximating the eloquence of Thomas Wolfe." *At the Crossing* is one Louise particularly loathed. Is that why she chose to ignore my dedication?

Louise!

Her moods changed at breathtaking speed. Her opinions were whimsical, profound, irritating, sublime. Much of it to be taken with more than a dash of salt.

As early as 1966, my friend was hoping to be published in book form. Although feigning indifference. She asked me to copy my Steichen original and I complied with two fine copies.

LULU in Hollywood by Louise Brooks was published by Knopf in 1982, comprising 109 carefully crafted pages.

She and I met at a good time for both of us. We shared not only a love of toys but a respect for writing. Where you roll up your sleeves—and write and *write again*. And polish and prune until you get to the essential truth.

The Louise I admired was not Lulu, the love 'em and leave 'em girl.

The Louise Brooks I loved and missed was the middle-aged fighter who called me Stink Pot.

Photo by HORST, Rochester, 1978.

Afterword

In 1959, two years after I'd served with Isak Dinesen and the year after I met Louise Brooks in Denmark, I was in The Big Apple to visit with my literary agent.

Somehow I encountered actor Zachary Scott and his wife Ruth Ford, who were most generous. They lived at The Dakota, the building where Leonard Bernstein resided and where John Lennon would be shot. I mentioned I'd been amanuensis to Isak Dinesen who was also in town.

"We're going to a lunch for her," Zachary remarked. Syncronicity! "She wants to meet Pearl Buck. Come along. And you can get re-acquainted."

If not the exact invitation, it's close enough.

I knew, through Dinesen's friend Clara Svendsen, that the Baroness despised Pearl Buck. Miss Buck received the Nobel Prize. Dinesen did not. No wonder she wanted to stare her in the face.

I had no wish to relive my painful experience with Dinesen, however curiosity got the better of me.

The luncheon was at the Fifth Avenue home of some banking magnate as I recall. We all sat at a very long table. I slouched down in my chair, hidden between Zachary and Ruth.

Jan Wahl at Toledo grade school, 1978.

The two grand ladies were seated at opposite ends of our table as proper literary royalty. The Baroness dropped names of those celebrities who paid or were about to pay homage to her: Marilyn Monroe, Truman Capote, Hemingway, e. e. cummings, Arthur Miller.

She seemed to glower at Pearl Buck who sat graciously silent, intent on catching each richly-flavored sentence. The two had not yet communicated.

With apologies, Buck announced she must depart early to catch a train to Connecticut to prepare dinner for her children. Like Josephine Baker, she had a rainbow tribe from all over the world.

Pearl Buck was gray-haired, regally beautiful; Isak Dinesen a regal Danish troll in a turban. Miss Buck excused herself and departed without much fuss. Dinesen kept holding court non-stop, enthralling her captive audience.

All at once she broke her thought — I don't remember the subject, one lyrical insight seamlessly flowed into the next—to sigh, to observe: "So. *That* was Pearl Buck?"

Banishing the Nobel prize-winner to oblivion.

I have put this episode last because it says something about ego. And when I told it to Louise, her response was peals of laughter, musical and strong. The sound of that laughter still rings in my ears.

About the
Author

About the Author

JAN WAHL grew up in North-West Ohio where as a child he played piano on a radio program *The Kiddies Karnival*, accompanying Teresa Brewer. Next came the creation of traveling magic and puppet shows and shadowplays. Once he appeared onstage with magician Harry Blackstone.

At Cornell he studied under *Lolita*'s Vladimir Nabokov and in Denmark was invited by director Carl Theodor Dreyer to be part of the making of the now-classic film *Ordet*. He returned to Denmark to act as scribe to Isak Dinesen (*Out of Africa*) when she wrote *Last Tales*.

He has written over 100 books for children of all ages. His stories have been anthologized, animated or set to music. His awards include the Avery Hopwood, the Redbook, the Ohioana, the Parents Magazine, as well as a Coretta Scott King prize and the Youth Critics Prize at Bologna. He received The Christopher Medal in 1987.

In 1996 he was given a doctorate in Arts and Letters from Bowling Green State University where he often presents programs at the Dorothy and Lillian Gish Film Theater. He lives in Toledo, Ohio.

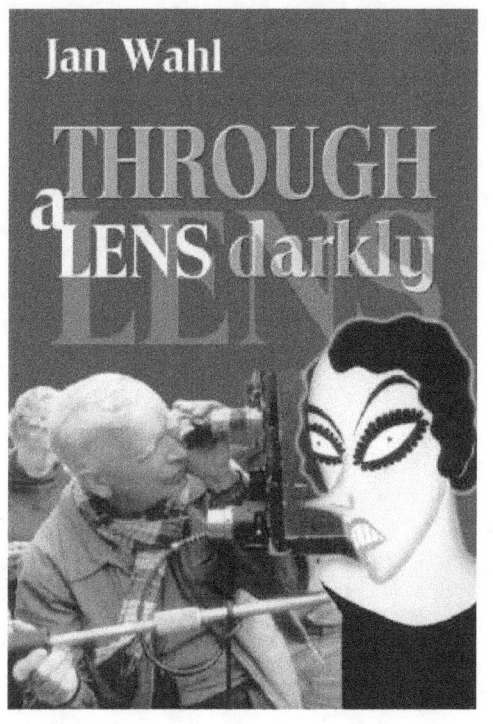
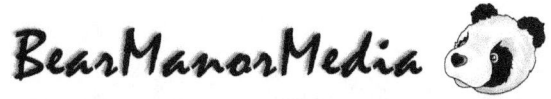

www.ingramcontent.com/pod-product-compliance
Lightning Source LLC
Chambersburg PA
CBHW070222030726
47505CB00006B/1788